THE ANCIENT
WORLD AT WORK

ANCIENT CULTURE AND SOCIETY

General Editor

M. I. FINLEY

Reader in Ancient Social and Economic
History in the University of Cambridge

C. MOSSÉ   The Ancient World at Work
R. M. OLGIVIE   The Romans and their Gods
B. H. WARMINGTON   Nero: Reality and Legend
M. I. FINLEY   Early Greece: the Bronze and Archaic Ages
Other titles in preparation

THE ANCIENT WORLD AT WORK

CLAUDE MOSSÉ

*Professor of Ancient History at the
Centre Universitaire Expérimental, Vincennes*

Translated from the French by
JANET LLOYD

1969
CHATTO & WINDUS
LONDON

Published by
Chatto & Windus Ltd
40 William IV Street
London WC2

*

Clarke, Irwin & Co. Ltd
Toronto

*First published as 'Le Travail en Grèce et à Rome' in
the series 'Que sais-je?' by Presses Universitaires de
France, 108 Boulevard Saint-Germain, Paris, in 1966
This edition first published 1969*

SBN 7011 1437 1 (hardback)
SBN 7011 1453 3 (paperback)

Printed in Great Britain by
Butler & Tanner Ltd,
Frome and London

CONTENTS

Acknowledgements

The author and publishers are grateful to the following for permission to quote from copyright material: Clarendon Press, Oxford, for Aristotle: *Politics* translated by E. Barker; William Heinemann Ltd and Harvard University Press for Cato: *De Agricultura* translated by W. D. Hooper and H. B. Ash, Cicero: *De Officiis* translated by W. Miller, Columella: *De Re Rustica* translated by E. S. Forster and E. Heffner, Herodotus: *III* and *V* translated by A. D. Godley, Hesiod: *Works and Days* translated by H. G. Evelyn-White, Isocrates: *Areopagitica* translated by G. Norlin, Pliny the Younger: *Letters* translated by W. Melmoth, Pliny the Elder: *Natural History* translated by D. E. Eichholz, Plutarch: *Tiberius Gracchus* translated by B. Perrin, Polybius: *Histories* translated by W. R. Paton, Thucydides: *I* and *II* translated by C. Foster-Smith, Xenophon: *Cyropaedia* translated by W. Miller, *Oeconomicus* and *Ways and Means* translated by E. C. Marchant, all in *The Loeb Classical Library*; George Bell Ltd for Aristophanes: *Ecclesiazusae* and *Plutus* translated by B. B. Rogers; Editions A & J Picard & Cie for Roland Martin: *Manuel D'Architecture Grecque*.

Plate I is reproduced by permission of K. D. White and the Cambridge University Press, Plates II and V The Mansell Collection, London, Plate III The Ashmolean Museum, Oxford, Plate IV Staatlichen Antikensammlungen, Munich.

PLATES

MAPS

(Drawn by Denys Baker)

SOME DATES FOR ORIENTATION

B.C.	*c.* 1200	End of Mycenaean civilisation
	c. 750	Beginning of Greek 'colonisation' of the west
	c. 625	Invention of coinage
	594	Archonship of Solon in Athens
	545–510	Tyranny of Pisistratids in Athens
	509	Establishment of Roman Republic
	508	Democracy introduced at Athens
	490–479	Persian wars
	431–404	Peloponnesian War
	429	Death of Pericles
	338	Defeat of Athens by Philip II of Macedon
	336–323	Alexander the Great
	272	Capture of Tarentum completes Roman conquest of Italy
	264–241	First Punic War
	218–201	Second Punic War
	168	Final defeat of Macedon by Rome
	c. 134–131	First Sicilian slave revolt
	133	Tribunate of Tiberius Gracchus
	c. 104–100	Second Sicilian slave revolt
	81–79	Dictatorship of Sulla
	73–71	Revolt of Spartacus
	46–44	Dictatorship of Caesar
	31	Battle of Actium gives Octavian (Augustus) sole power
A.D.	14	Death of Augustus
	180	Death of Marcus Aurelius
	284–305	Reign of Diocletian
	330	Foundation of Constantinople

PREFACE

Essentially this book is a translation of *Le Travail en Grèce et à Rome*, published in Paris in 1966. I have revised the original in order to clarify the analysis still further for the layman, in particular by introducing more concrete examples into an argument which was at times too abstract in the French original (which also lacked illustrations). A completely new bibliography has been prepared for English readers.

I am most grateful to Mrs Janet Lloyd who kindly took on the ungrateful assignment of preparing the translation; to J. W. Roberts of Eton College who read the manuscript and made many useful comments; and above all to my friend Moses Finley who worked closely with me in the preparation of this edition, and whose suggestions have been of the greatest value to me.

CLAUDE MOSSÉ

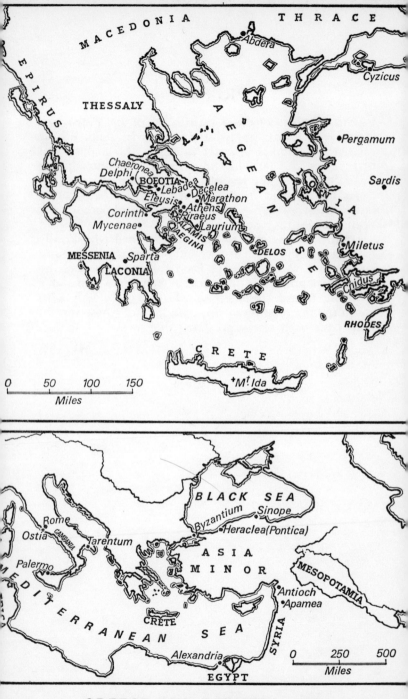

GREECE AND WESTERN ASIA

Introduction

WORK has been idealised first by Christianity and then by Socialism: 'Thou shalt earn thy bread by the sweat of thy brow,' 'Workers of the world, unite.' These two phrases sum up an attitude of mind in which work has an absolute value as a source either of redemption or of justification. Man is condemned to work for his living, but the worker sublimates this sentence and it becomes a source of glory and pride for him. In the world of socialism, intellectuals consider themselves primarily as 'workers', and both in the East and in the West women see in work the means of their emancipation. Laziness and idleness are vices or privileges to be destroyed. The reduction of working hours is, of course, the ideal to which men aspire, but it is an ideal which was unknown in our earlier history, and in the modern world dominated by the notion of profit it chiefly implies economic recession, half-hidden poverty, and partial or total unemployment.

In antiquity, too, men had invented their Golden Age. But instead of projecting it into the future they mourned for it as a bygone past. And labour, for them, appeared as a sentence to which no redeeming value was attached. This explains its lack of importance in the eyes of writers and thinkers, and the lowly position to which society relegated its workers. Idleness was not a vice, but an ideal to which every gentleman aspired, and which was praised by wise men too.

Given these conditions, it may well be imagined what difficulties face the historian attempting to reconstruct a picture of work and labour in Greece and Rome. It is an attempt which other writers have already made, and I should like to acknowledge my debt to them. What I have tried to avoid is a 118-page summary of earlier studies of the subject. Furthermore, this study is largely restricted to the Graeco-Roman world. It does not cover

1

the immense eastern empires with their own special problems, which were only partially affected by the Greek and Roman conquests, nor does it attempt to consider the Celtic or Germanic areas which were integrated into the Roman Empire only at a late date.

At the centre of this study is the ancient city. This original political structure started to develop in the eighth century B.C. and reached a first climax with the flowering of Greek civilisation in the fifth century, and a second with the expansion of Rome in the third and second centuries B.C. The Roman Empire was at first only a federation of cities and territories grouped around the mother city, the *Urbs*. When, from the time of Diocletian onwards, it increasingly took the form of a truly unified state, ancient civilisation had practically come to an end. It is therefore within the framework of the city that we shall study the problem of labour. Because the character of the city changed very little, in theory at least, in the course of six centuries, we shall study the problems in cross-section, with the aim of revealing both the permanent features and the specific characteristics of work in classical antiquity.

PART ONE

LABOUR AND SOCIETY

I

Social and Political Conditions

THE Graeco-Roman world, the world of the city-state, introduced a new social structure in the Mediterranean world. Brilliant civilisations had developed and flourished in the Near East before the Greek civilisation. But even where the king was not considered to be actually a god, the social and political structure of all of them was determined by the divine origins of royal power which made the king the master of the land and of men. The royal palace was accordingly also the centre where all decisions were taken, whether political, military or economic. There are obvious differences between the societies of Mesopotamia, Egypt and Asia Minor, but in none of them did the community of free men play any part at all in political activity. The originality of the city-state lies in this participation of the community of free men, the citizens, in political decisions.

The city made its appearance, as a specific form of society or state, towards the end of the eighth century B.C. It is possible that there was an embryonic form of 'democracy' in Mycenaean civilisation, but, as in the towns of the ancient Near East, the royal palace was still the place where, in the last resort, all military, political, religious and economic decisions were taken. The Mycenaean civilisation disappeared abruptly in about the twelfth century B.C., and then followed the obscure years of the Dark Age of Greece (c. 1150–c.750 B.C.). We know nothing of the political history of this period, but both the Homeric poems and archaeological discoveries suggest the existence of a society dominated by an aristocracy of warriors who were the masters of the land and of its flocks, if not of the men who cultivated it. During the eighth and seventh centuries there were gradual new

5

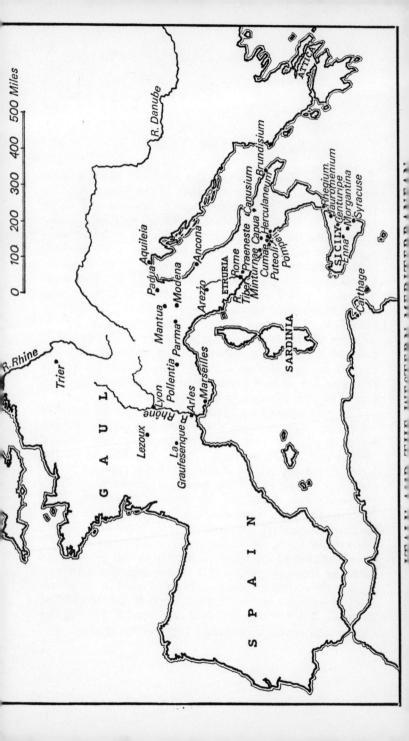

ITALY AND THE WESTERN MEDITERRANEAN

developments, the stages of which we can generally follow only through the mute evidence of archaeology or the more or less reconstructed accounts of later writers. After conflicts which were sometimes violent, and which frequently led to periods of one-man rule, called 'tyranny' by the Greeks, a civic community was established, controlling its own military forces and its own sovereignty, which it delegated, either entirely or in part, to certain of its members, selected by birth, by wealth or simply by lot. This is, of course, a schematic account and there were many variants. Moreover this evolution did not take place everywhere at the same pace. However, it is undeniable that a new form of state emerged which created among its members close ties which often found expression in civic patriotism.

Let us concentrate on the two well-known examples, Sparta and Athens. In appearance they are fundamentally different. In fact, however, Sparta, like Athens, developed a constitution in which the community of *Homoioi*, or 'equal Spartiates', was the repository of national sovereignty. It is true that the circumstances peculiar to the history of Sparta, especially the two great wars with Messenia, gave this community a rather unusual character which survived, in theory at least, for centuries, and which was to give rise to the 'Spartan legend': its military upbringing, the absence of any private property or even of any private life, and, as a corollary, the stress laid on the communal institutions such as the *syssitia*, the messes where the Spartans assembled to consume their famous black broth. There are still many obscurities about what Spartan life was really like, and the ancients were fascinated by it just as we are today. One fact nevertheless emerges: the importance of the civic community which constituted the state, even though it did delegate almost all its powers to limited organs such as the *Gerousia* or council of elders, and the college of the five annual magistrates, the *Ephors*.

In Attica, the community of citizens gained control of

the state at a later date. At the beginning of the seventh century B.C. only the *Eupatrids*, the aristocrats, could hold office. Here too it is difficult to form a clear idea of the changes which gradually led to the affirmation of the sovereignty of the *demos*, after many conflicts involving antagonists about whom we often know very little. Athenian tradition has handed down to us the names of Solon, Pisistratus, and Cleisthenes, who, during the sixth century, created the conditions making this sovereignty possible, although their personal motives were in some respects widely different. Solon, the 'Liberator', listened to the complaints of the peasants of Attica who were forced to pay heavy rents to the Eupatrids, and were threatened with servitude for debt. He did away with the *horoi*[1] which 'enslaved' the land and forbade a man to mortgage himself or his children. However, despite the reputation which he later acquired in the tradition, he did not really create democracy, and it is almost certain that the assembly of citizens, if it existed at all at that time, was composed only of those among the Athenians who were capable of providing their own armour as hoplites, or heavy infantry. Pisistratus, in his turn, favoured the small peasants. He also admitted to the civic community people who until then had been excluded because of their place of origin or their occupation. But by assuming sole responsibility for the affairs of the city, and by sending the citizens back to their private business, he in effect stripped the civic community of its sovereignty. It was Cleisthenes who, 'by admitting the *demos* to his *hetairia*', as Herodotus puts it (V, 66), created the real conditions of popular sovereignty. The *hetairiai* were political associations which grouped the

[1] In classical Greece, the *horoi* were the stone boundary posts which were placed round a piece of mortgaged land and which generally bore an inscription giving the name of the holder of the debt claim, and sometimes the value of the land and the total of the sum owing. It is this same term which is used by Solon when he refers to his liberation of the soil and peasantry of Attica, in the poem quoted by Aristotle (*Constitution of Athens* XII, 4).

8

associates (*hetairoi*) around a politician whom they supported and whose clients they became. Thus the entire *demos* became supporters of Cleisthenes, and in exchange received from him the means of really exercising sovereign power. By creating the deme, a political parish which included within it all the men from one territorial district without any distinctions of birth, and by making the demes the basis for the entire political organisation of the city, he created true democracy.

It would be possible to trace the stages in a similar evolution in other cities in the Greek world, where tyranny often contributed towards hastening the fall of the aristocracies and the emergence of the *demos*, even though, as was often the case, the sovereignty of the *demos* remained purely theoretical and was delegated to more or less restricted councils, while in Sparta and elsewhere kingship survived with more or less effective powers. In the Classical period Greek political writers were fond of drawing distinctions between different types of *politeiai*, or political constitutions. But however important they may have been, and however often they were a source of conflict, these differences always existed within a common context, the sovereign political community.

We can trace the evolution of the Roman Republic within this same context. From the moment that the plebeians gained official recognition, at the beginning of the fifth century B.C., the *comitia tributa* and the Senate became the joint guardians of sovereignty. Right up to the end of the Roman Empire, the famous sign *S.P.Q.R.* (*senatus populusque Romanus*) symbolised the reality of this sovereignty, even though, in fact, at the height of the Republic it was considerably undermined by the subtle manœuvre of dividing the citizens into different categories, and later, under the Empire, it was delegated to one absolute master.

Thus, the city-state appears as the specific framework of a sovereign community, the principle of which endured until the end of the Roman Empire. This is not

9

to say that the city-state remained unchanged throughout a thousand years of history. The ancient cities, often torn with internal dissension and threatened by enemies from without, were obliged to become integrated within larger entities—federations, kingdoms, and finally the Empire which was created by one of them, Rome. But the fiction of a 'political' life survived both in the Greek cities of the Hellenistic world and in the towns of the Roman provinces, where, even as the Empire was crumbling beneath the onslaught of the barbarians, the urban *curiae* still continued to elect judges and to vote on decrees.

The history of labour cannot be considered in the abstract. It is bound up with the evolution of social relationships which determine the most obvious material conditions of work. Once again we must isolate the experience of Sparta. The Spartan constitution depended upon social relations established once and for all: the 'Equals' each received an allotment of land cultivated by helots belonging to the community. These allotments were inalienable and nothing, in theory, could alter the original distribution made by the legendary Lycurgus. In actual fact, Spartan 'communism' was theoretical rather than real. The city would have had to cut itself off from the rest of the Greek world in order to maintain it. This was hardly possible, and from the fourth century B.C. onwards Sparta was the scene of disturbances caused by an increasingly unequal distribution of the land; in the third century attempts at 'revolution' even involved the helots. Needless to say, these proved abortive, and the Roman conquest of Greece in the second century ensured that they would remain impossible in the future.

The social history of the other cities is more complex and more closely related to the problem of labour. Our sources are mostly literary, with supporting or complementary evidence from inscriptions, and often they permit us only to form hypotheses or approximations. There are no statistics, and the seeming juridical precision of the terminology is often misleading. We shall devote ourselves to Athens, as it alone provides us with an example which we can follow with some continuity.

As always, the beginnings are obscure. However, there are indications that at the end of the seventh century and the beginning of the sixth most of the population lived off the land. When late in the seventh Cylon tried to seize the Acropolis and establish a tyranny, the people, according to Thucydides (I, 127, 7), 'came in their multitudes from the countryside' in order to oppose him and to support Megacles, the archon or chief magistrate. And some years later, it was the gravity of the agrarian crisis which brought about the intervention of Solon. Unfortunately we have very little information about the origins of this agrarian crisis, and what we have comes from later writers whose picture is often inexact.

Who, in particular, were the *hektemoroi*, the peasants who were bound to pay such heavy rents to the landowners? Were they tenants or former landowners whom poverty had driven into servitude? We must confess that we do not know. We must, moreover, beware the modern theories which use terms like 'property' and 'debts' and a whole anachronistic modern vocabulary to describe a situation which was in fact quite different. One thing remains certain: when Solon 'freed' the land from the *horoi*, he did away with the class of *hektemoroi*, but he did not resolve the agrarian crisis. He himself admits to having resisted those who were demanding a redistribution of the land. Although land was at that time the principal form of wealth and agriculture the principal occupation, the possessors of the land and those who actually farmed it were not necessarily the same people. Social inequality was still the fundamental reality as is shown by the division of the citizens into four qualifying classes: the *pentakosiomedimnoi* (those whose harvests exceeded 500 measures of grain, wine or oil), the *hippeis* (300 measures), the *zeugitai* (200 measures), and the *thetes*, who included all those who had no property and lived by their labour.

11

However, during the sixth century the situation changed. Solon's laws on inheritance[1] favoured not only the mobility of land-ownership but also the division of the land into smaller allotments. But above all, in a situation in which aristocratic factions were struggling with each other to seize political power, the rural *demos* found allies among the artisans in the city and in the villages. These were the *demiourgoi*, whose number must have been increasing; apart from the smiths who manufactured arms, and the carpenters, there were more and more potters whose wares were increasingly in demand all along the Mediterranean coast. Most of these were not Athenians, hence they had no political rights, not even the right to bear the arms they were producing. Nevertheless, they constituted a force whose strength was beginning to be felt. There is some doubt about the authenticity of the compromise agreement of 580 B.C. which is said to have admitted two *demiourgoi* to the board of archons along with three farmers and five Eupatrids, and it is an exaggeration to make Pisistratus the champion of the artisans, as some historians have done. What happened was that, being at the head of one of the opposing factions, he called upon the assistance of the *demos* in order to set himself up as tyrant. Once in power after 545 B.C. (having twice had to give it up before that date), Pisistratus favoured the farmers by giving them loans of seed-corn and tools, and possibly also by dividing land which he had confiscated from his opponents. The great building projects which he undertook in order to lend greater prestige to his tyranny attracted the best artisans to Athens, and at the same time he laid the basis for the city's future military and commercial power. However, his sons, who succeeded him, did not possess his breadth of vision. So when the exiled aristocrats overthrew Hippias with the aid of Sparta, the *demos* did nothing to help him. But then,

[1] In particular the one which authorised a man to dispose of his land by will if there was no legitimate heir.

when the quarrels between the various aristocratic clans which had momentarily died down sprang up again, the *demos* proved so strong that the Eupatrid Cleisthenes turned to it as his ally against his enemy who had the military support of Sparta. This alliance was sanctioned by his creation of the Athenian democracy.

The Athenian democracy of the fifth century was the most fully achieved political régime known in the ancient world. It was not free from conflicts, to be sure, at least until the strong personality of Pericles had made its impression. At that moment Athens did achieve an exceptional degree of political stability. However, its fragility should not be overlooked. Pericles was prominent but not dominant until the ostracism of Thucydides, son of Melesias, in about 446. In the years immediately preceding the Peloponnesian War his enemies brought lawsuits against his friends. In 430 or 429 he was temporarily removed from office. The political stability of the régime depended essentially upon the remarkable personality of the man who had taken control of the city's fate. Once he was gone, it too vanished, as can be seen by the two oligarchic revolutions which, first in 411 following the disastrous expedition to Sicily, and again in 404 after the defeat, were able to overthrow democracy. Nevertheless, the extraordinary prosperity of Athens, bound up with the imperial power which she held over the Aegean world, did make possible a very real social stability which found expression in the splendid flowering of Athenian culture. We can try to analyse the elements composing this social equilibrium. On the eve of the Peloponnesian War there were about 40,000 adult male citizens of Athens, of whom more than half possessed at least the zeugite qualification. The settlement of 10,000 poor citizens in the cleruchies, the military colonies set up by Athens on the territories of the recalcitrant cities in her Empire and also on a few islands which actually belonged to her, had considerably reduced the number of citizens in the lowest class, the *thetes*. Most thetes had some occupation which assured them of a livelihood, or even a small parcel of land. When, following the Peloponnesian War, a certain Phormisius proposed restricting citizenship to those who were owners of real property, no matter how small a holding, the orator Lysias, whose speech (34) helped to defeat the bill, complained that this would deprive 5,000 Athenians of their citizenship. Even supposing that war, plague, and other disasters of every kind had reduced the body of citizens by one quarter, it is clear that at least five-sixths of the Athenians were landowners of some kind, however modest.

This is still not to say that every landowner was a farmer. The artisan might well own a small garden within the city itself, and in the rural demes this must have been the general rule. This garden might well supplement the family budget, with the wife taking to market whatever vegetables or other produce not needed to feed the family. In fact, although in the fifth century land was still the most noble form of wealth, and although agriculture was still the main occupation of the greatest number of citizens, the artisan class, encouraged by the extraordinary commercial and maritime development of the city, had increased in importance. The needs of a growing population, further increased by large numbers of foreigners and slaves from many lands, had to be met. Furthermore, craftsmen were in demand for supplying the trade in vases, coins and arms, and in the Piraeus the docks and naval yards were humming with activity. It is true that many of these manufacturing and commercial activities were not carried out by citizens, but it would be wrong to suppose that the metics (*metoikoi*, free Greeks from other cities, permanently resident in Athens) and slaves were responsible for them all. If they had been, it would be difficult to understand Pericles' declaration (Thucydides II, 40, 2) that a simple craftsman could understand politics as well as anyone, or Socrates' gibes at an assembly dominated by carpenters, smiths and fullers. Unfortunately it is impossible to estimate precisely the size of the different sections of the society. There have been endless arguments over attempts to establish the number of slaves living in Athens in the Classical period. The figure of 400,000, given by an ancient author, Athenaeus of Naucratis, reporting the results of a census supposed to have been taken in Athens at the end of the fourth century, is clearly too high, especially if we compare it with the number of free men (31,000 according to the same census). On the other hand the estimates put forward by some modern authors, based upon more or less valid criteria, are sometimes exaggeratedly low. The best we can do is to assume that at the time of the greatest development of slavery in Athens, the number of slaves was, at the most, 150,000 or perhaps 200,000 (including women and children). There are not likely to have been more than about 15,000 adult male metics at the time when they were being drawn to Athens by its wealth and by the financial and commercial importance of the Piraeus. Most of these resident foreigners were merchants or specialised craftsmen. As for the slaves, they were to be found working in the fields as well as in workshops, with bankers, in the arsenals, in the docks, and on public works.

The Peloponnesian War was to have a drastic effect on this stability. It was caused as much by the unbounded ambition of Athens as by the opposition to this ambition on the part of Sparta and, even more, Corinth, and it soon proved disastrous for everybody concerned. Land was laid waste, houses burnt or destroyed, whole populations massacred or sold into slavery. The list of disasters which afflicted Greece at this time is unending, but more terrible even than the war was the plague which in Athens carried off more than a quarter of the population. Thucydides has given an unforgettable account (II, 47–54) of the disaster whose victims increased in number week by week, and which undermined the bases of morality and religion, destroyed all human dignity and reduced men to the level of beasts. Among its last victims was Pericles, who had accepted the conflict, confident

15

that it would strengthen the power of Athens. In actual fact, after being conducted in increasingly disastrous conditions by his successors, it eventually brought about Athens' downfall.

After the Peloponnesian War, and following two oligarchic revolutions which enabled the bitterest adversaries of democracy to act unchecked against its real interests, Athens was still not completely crushed and did enjoy fine periods in the fourth century, but the social equilibrium which had enabled the Athenians in the fifth century to dominate the Aegean world was doomed from that time onwards. The peasants were most severely affected, as is eloquently illustrated in Aristophanes' plays. Already in 421, in the *Peace*, he portrayed the peasants, weary of war, uniting to free the goddess of peace. But it is especially in the later plays, the *Ecclesiazusae* and the *Plutus*, that he laid bare the misery of the peasants in the aftermath of war. With fields uncultivated, olive-groves and vineyards destroyed, and flocks slaughtered, the small peasant of Attica was left with no resources. It takes several years for a vineyard to recover, or for an olive tree to bear fruit. The cultivation of cereals provided barely enough to live on, and anyway more and more wheat was being imported from abroad. True, the ruined peasant could raise a loan in order to attempt to rebuild his life, but this involved great risks, for he had to give all his possessions as security.

Contrary to what has sometimes been asserted, the poverty-stricken small farmers of Attica did not in fact often resort to this expedient. A study of the stones on which mortgage-bonds were recorded and publicised has shown that most of them concerned holdings of a considerable size, and we know further that in order to meet the obligations of a liturgy,[1] wealthy people had no com-

[1] A liturgy was a responsibility, accepted as an honour, which the city entrusted to a rich citizen. It involved the training and equipment of a chorus, the maintenance of a trireme, etc. During the fourth century, these responsibilities, particularly the trier-

punction in mortgaging their possessions. Some small farmers were, of course, less affected than others, but when he could no longer gain a living from his land, the small peasant sold it and came to live in the town where he made some kind of a living from petty jobs together with the various salaries (*misthoi*) that he could earn as wages or as remuneration for attending sessions of the *Ecclesia* (city assembly), and the grant for entertainments (*theorikon*), which had, in effect, become an allowance. He very seldom remained as a tenant on the land which he no longer owned. These uncultivated plots of land, sold cheap by the peasants who had their backs to the wall, were bought up by clever speculators who put them under cultivation again and then resold them to some *nouveau riche* who was anxious to rise in the social hierarchy by becoming a landowner. Xenophon's *Oeconomicus* gives us valuable information about these speculations which made it possible for some people to amass fortunes. The banker Pasion, an ex-slave, could congratulate himself on owning land to the value of twenty talents. The speeches of the Attic orators, particularly of the second half of the fourth century B.C., are an especially eloquent testimony to the mobility of wealth which was at this time one of the aspects of social instability heralding the city's downfall.

The peasants, however, were not the only ones to be affected. During the fourth century production in the ceramic workshops slowed down considerably, and after a brief revival in the sixties of the century the mines at Laurium went into permanent decline. The foreign merchants deserted the Piraeus. Only the Athenian coinage, the famous 'little owls', still enjoyed general confidence and made it possible for Athens to maintain an impressive operational fleet, and to recruit mercenaries for the constant wars which she was forced to wage. Even in 340, two years before the defeat at Chaeronea

---

archy, had become increasingly onerous, and some people had to borrow money in order to meet them.

finally ruined Athenian ambitions to dominate the Aegean, Athens could still muster an army and a fleet capable of putting up opposition to Macedonia. Greek liberty came to an end in 338, when not only Athens but the whole of Greece was defeated.

With Greece under the domination of Alexander, and later on his successors, the Ptolemies and the Antigonids, Athens finally gave up all claims to power. Although poverty-stricken and wretched even in her countryside, she could still present an illusion of splendour thanks to her writers and artists. But increasingly these were financed by foreign sovereigns, in particular by the kings of Pergamum who were to adorn Athens with the last of her great monuments. The Piraeus had at last lost its position as the great commercial centre of the Aegean, first to Rhodes, and later to Delos and Alexandria. Painted vases were no longer produced, and the 'little owls' of Laurium were being superseded by the coinage of the Hellenistic dynasties. Athens had become no more than a museum-town and was soon to become the university town for rich educated Romans. And although a few lucky Athenians like the famous Herodes Atticus could, even under the Roman Empire, pose as patrons, most of the descendants of the heroes of Marathon and Salamis lived wretchedly on the scarce products of their land, and the glorious *demos* of Athens could no longer even pretend to claim a privileged position, for this was now held by the *populus Romanus*.

It is very interesting to study the fortunes of Rome after considering the decline of Athens, for the beginning of Athens' decline coincides closely with the beginning of the remarkable venture which turned the little city in Latium and its population of peasants into the masters of the world. Originally nothing seemed to mark Rome out for its destiny. Certainly its site was excellent, but it suffered from the disadvantage that its access to the sea was no more than mediocre. Its neighbours were either powerful like the Etruscans, or belligerent as were the mountain people of the Apennines. Both its agricultural and its industrial resources were unimpressive. It would be fruitless to try to understand why all these factors which do not seem to herald an extraordinary destiny should have in the event produced the greatest Empire that men have ever known and whose influence is still felt more than fifteen centuries after its eclipse. Anyway, our intention is the more modest one of trying to assess the place of labour in this history and to determine the social conditions which affected its development.

Since Rome, even more than Athens, was originally a city of peasants, its religion reflected this for a long time, and its laws were also deeply affected, as were the legends which make up its earliest history. The *paterfamilias* was first and foremost a farmer, and only in second place a soldier and a citizen, and Cincinnatus is truly the model of those first Romans who were never entirely to be forgotten, and who returned, when the wars were ended and the city saved, to till their fields. In the times of the Gracchi and the agrarian crisis there was a tendency to idealise that past age which had in actual fact had its own disturbances and conflicts. But although there did exist then a very real inequality maintained by the electoral qualifications, and although the old patrician families could take pride in possessing the best land in Latium and knew how to turn the earliest Roman conquests to their own advantage, nevertheless the land was divided up into numerous allotments, among a large number of small landowners. They were fiercely attached to their land and to the gods who protected it, and were ready to die to defend it and hand it down to their heirs. There were few craftsmen then, only those who were indispensable to this people of farmer-soldiers. There were no traders apart from a few foreigners, Greeks or Phoenicians, who were rather despised and held at a distance. In this world there was very little trade; coinage did not make its appearance until later, and even then it at first took the form of clumsy bronze coins.

Nevertheless, this peasant people gradually made itself master of central Italy, first in self-defence and then

c

finding that one victory led to yet another. At the dawn of the third century B.C., while the brilliant civilisation of the Hellenistic kingdoms was flourishing in the East, Rome was making contact with the most Western representatives of this civilisation, with the Greek city of Tarentum and with Pyrrhus, the king of Epirus who rather saw himself as the Alexander of the West. Rome had already had contacts with the Greek world, both in the West, as at Marseilles, and also in the East, but the acquisition of Greek cities in southern Italy gave these contacts a new importance. Above all it led Rome on to commit herself to the venture of the Punic Wars and later the wars in the East.

This is not the place to retrace their history. All that concern us are the effects of these wars on the development of Roman society. The effects were considerable, upsetting the entire traditional structure of the city. In the first place, Italy was inundated with riches of all kinds: plunder, slaves, silver (both coined and bullion). This wealth was certainly not divided equally among those who had fought for it. The generals took the largest share, and among the soldiers the *cives Romani*, the Roman citizens, took precedence over the other Italians, which naturally created an uneasy situation. Moreover, only a small proportion of this wealth contributed towards enriching Italy in any real sense, by being used to increase production. The small peasants returned after long years spent away from their land, laden indeed with booty, but once this was spent, they had to get down to work again. It was a hard task to work the fields which had lain uncultivated for so long, and the habits acquired from riches quickly obtained during the victorious wars made such an effort all the harder to bear.

Meantime the acquisition of the rich wheat lands of Sicily, North Africa and Asia brought to Italy a profusion of cheap grain which put out of the question any Italian revival in the cultivation of cereals. It was better to devote the land to a more scientific and profitable type of farming and so the culture of the vine and the olive was preferred to grain farming. For such a conversion one needed capital, an extensive property, and a fairly large labour force. The wars had indeed thrown on to the Italian market large numbers of captives who could be bought very cheaply. But then the farmer had to be able to feed them and employ them. Thus in Rome and in other Italian cities only a minority could really profit from the new economic conditions by developing a scientifically based agriculture which was inspired by the agronomic treatises produced in Carthage or in the Hellenistic capitals. The great mass of poverty-stricken Roman peasants, drawn by the memory of an easier life, streamed into the towns, while large estates were developed through the legal acquisition of uncultivated land, and also by the more or less open seizure of common land, the *ager publicus*, which was transformed into vast areas of pasture.[1]

These changes evoked a reaction from some quarters. The aim of the Gracchi was to reintroduce small peasant-holdings by sharing out the *ager publicus* in such a way as to recreate for the Roman Republic the solid basis formed by the class of peasant-soldiers which had been its glory. The Gracchi failed, not so much because they clashed with the privileged classes as because the Roman conquests had made any return to an antiquated past impossible. Actually, it never occurred to Tiberius Gracchus, still less to Caius, to forego the benefits of con-quest, as is proved by Tiberius' acceptance of Attalus III's bequest to Rome of the rich Asiatic provinces, and by the plans of Caius Gracchus to set up an African colony on Carthaginian soil. There could no longer be any question of reconstructing that community of small farmers of which the Republic had been composed before the wars in the third and second centuries B.C. Besides the conquests had not only upset the social equilibrium within the city: by placing considerable

[1] We shall discuss this problem in greater detail in Part II, Chapter 4.

wealth in the hands of the Romans and Italians they turned these farmers into the most skilful businessmen of the Mediterranean world. During the second century in Delos, which was then one of the foremost markets in the Mediterranean, the *Romaioi* far outstripped the other groups of traders—Syrians, Phoenicians, Greeks, Egyptians—both in the volume of trade products and also in their capital gains. In Rome itself an increasingly Hellenised 'bourgeoisie' was growing accustomed to the refinements of art and culture, and found its needs constantly expanding, and this was a considerable impetus to the development of industries and particularly those that catered for luxuries.

The consequences of these economic and social changes upon the political situation were civil war, the destruction of the Roman people as a political body, the struggles for political power between the generals, and the eventual triumph of the cleverest of them who understood how to reconcile the Roman tradition with the new problems of an immense Mediterranean empire. Under the constitution which Augustus worked out, the *populus Romanus* retained its privileges. It is true that its ranks had been swollen by almost the entire population of Italy when Roman citizenship had been given to them during the struggles of the first century B.C., and the granting of citizenship was to become increasingly generous during the first two centuries of the Empire, leading up to Caracalla's *constitutio Antoniniana*. (The emperor Caracalla's edict, made at the end of A.D. 211 or the beginning of 212, conferred Roman citizenship upon all free men in the Empire.) Nevertheless, the people of the *urbs*, the city of Rome, still held, by reason of its very cohesion, a special place in the Empire. Theoretically, the sovereignty still resided there, and when the frontier troops began to nominate emperors, the latter still thought it necessary to have themselves consecrated by the people and the Senate.

This fiction was all the more remarkable because Italy had ceased to be the vital centre of the Mediterranean

world. Economically she was declining in the face of competition from the provinces. The arboriculture which had
been developed to such an extent was no longer profitable on account of the high cost of labour, and the loss of
markets. Oil from Africa and Spain cost less than oil
produced in Italy, and was tending more and more to
take its place. For this reason the medium-sized property
which had been ideal for the development of a scientific
agriculture, such as Cato had described, was in its turn
disappearing. But while the concentration of land into
latifundia was taking place, even these large estates were
proving economically unsound as is clearly shown by the
difficulties which Pliny the Younger refers to in his
correspondence (*cf*. Pliny, *Letters* III, 19: '. . . but partly
by the general calamity of the times, and partly by its
being thus stripped of labourers, the income of this
estate is reduced, and consequently its value'). Slaves were
expensive and were becoming increasingly scarce
because wars of conquest had come to an end and the
pax Romana established a relative stability throughout
the Empire. So there was a gradual return to farming in
smaller units. However, both tenants and sharecroppers
paying rent in kind were difficult to find, for careers in
the army or in the bureaucracy offered more attractions
than hard work on the land. There were larger and
larger stretches of *agri deserti*, the abandoned fields
which from that time dominated the Italian countryside.
In an attempt to counter this irreversible tendency, the
emperors tried many measures, such as loans, propa-
ganda, offers of all kinds of advantages—and eventually
from the end of the third century A.D. they fell back to
force, tying the peasant to the land which he cultivated,
and so preparing the way for the serfdom of the Middle
Ages.

It was also under duress that the skills which were indispensable to everyday life survived in Rome and in the
Italian towns. There, too, provincial competition was
making itself felt: the presence in Italy from the second
century A.D. of pottery from Lezoux and La Graufesen-

que in France illustrates the decline of Italian crafts-manship in the face of the massive influx of provincial products. The same could be said for the textile and metallurgical industries. The only crafts which continued to function, if not to flourish, were those which were necessary to feed a vociferous urban population. It was precisely these skills, baking, milling and so on, which were later, in the fourth century, to be strictly controlled by the emperors, who were anxious to maintain order in the largest town in the Empire.

Thus the example of Rome and Italy provides a complement to that of Athens, and we may now assess the effect of the social and political conditions on labour in antiquity. In each case we have a city based upon a community of small farmers who were free; both cities were caught up in external wars which enabled them to establish internal stability, but which at the same time brought about far-reaching changes in their social structure. Athens, however, was unable to create for herself an empire such as Rome slowly but surely built up. Thereafter Athens, defeated, wretched and poverty-stricken, reduced to the position of a museum-town, was no longer economically of the least importance, and the problems of labour in Greece became frozen in a permanently archaic condition. Rome, on the other hand, survived, and even at the moment that it was about to break under the onslaught of the barbarians it was preparing the way for a new ecumenical system. For that reason Rome remains to the end an important focal point for our topic. Late imperial Rome was a vast consumer, supplied at the expense of the provinces, a parasitical society with special labour problems arising from the need to support an idle and disorderly population which pretended to a large influence in the affairs of the Empire, which, for all its adherence to Christianity, was unenthusiastic about the ideal of work as preached by the Church. So deeply rooted in men's minds was the idea that work is unworthy of a free man.

2

The Idea of Work in Antiquity

IN antiquity, work was not assigned the moral value which it has gained from twenty centuries of Christianity, and from the birth of the Labour movement. The fact that manual labour was despised has seemed to many historians to be the natural corollary to slavery, and at the same time to explain the stagnation of techniques. There are many evidences that such an attitude existed. In his *Oeconomicus* (IV, 2, 3), Xenophon puts into Socrates' mouth words which leave no doubt about the matter: '. . . to be sure, the illiberal arts [*banausikai*], as they are called, are spoken against, and are, naturally enough, held in utter disdain in our states. For they spoil the bodies of the workmen and the foremen, forcing them to sit still and live indoors, and in some cases to spend the day at the fire. The softening of the body involves a serious weakening of the mind. Moreover, these so-called illiberal arts leave no spare time for attention to one's friends and city, so that those who follow them are reputed bad at dealing with friends and bad defenders of their country. In fact, in some of the states, and especially in those reputed warlike, it is not even lawful for any of the citizens to work at illiberal arts.' In his *Politics* (1329a 1–2), Aristotle recommends that the citizens should cultivate leisure for 'leisure is a necessity, both for growth in goodness and for the pursuit of political activities'. The same conception of *otium cum dignitate* appears as the ideal of life in Roman writers at the end of the Republic and the beginning of the Empire. It implied that work was an obstacle to such a life, and a degradation.

Xenophon's view has something in common with the epithet which Cicero used in his *De Officiis* (I, 42, 150) to describe the occupations of artisans: he called them *sordidi.* Isocrates had already carried this to its logical conclusion in his *Areopagitica* (26), where he had said that political rights should be confined 'to those citizens who could afford the time and possessed sufficient means'. The corollary to this is that all manual work must be carried out by slaves or by free men of a lower social standing.

But as we have already seen, such a situation really occurred only in Sparta. There, the citizen, being freed from all material cares by the work of the helots, devoted himself entirely to war, while any artisan work was the concern of those who lived in the cities of the *perioikoi*. Everywhere else in the Greek world, as in Italy under the Romans, the citizens included peasants who cultivated their own land, and others who gained their living by commerce or craftsmanship. Pericles proclaimed that, in Athens, in those 'of us who give attention chiefly to business, you will find no lack of insight into political matters' (Thucydides II, 40). The many memorials to the dead raised by rich artisans in the Roman world, especially in Italy and in Gaul, and ornamented by relief sculptures glorifying work and manual labour, also spring to mind. The inscriptions at Herculaneum and Pompeii reveal the existence of an urban 'bourgeoisie', composed of well-to-do artisans and shopkeepers. Even in Rome, in the later years of the Republic, there was a respected class of businessmen and artisans who, although they took no part in politics, nevertheless enjoyed some social standing as is shown by the inscriptions of the *collegia* to which they belonged.

Was it then only a small minority of intellectuals with their aristocratic prejudices who despised manual labour? The problem is more complex and can be approached only within its historical context. Two preliminary points must be made. The first is that except in a few systematic thinkers, such as Aristotle, work on the land does not incur this contempt, which is in fact only directed at the work of the artisan. 'Even stout-hearted warriors cannot live without the aid of workers . . . those who stock and cultivate the land,' says Xenophon in his *Oeconomicus* (IV, 15), and even Aristotle, who elsewhere praises complete idleness, says (*Politics*, 1318b 1): 'the first and best kind of populace is one of farmers; and there is thus no difficulty in constructing a democracy where the bulk of the people live by arable or pastoral farming.'

In Rome, the same spirit prompted the work of the agrarian reformers which can only be understood in the context of the moral and political renaissance which took place in the city. Three centuries after Xenophon, Cicero echoes his feelings when he writes (*De Officiis* I, 42): 'none is better than agriculture, none more profitable, none more delightful, none more becoming in a free man'.

Life in the fields strengthened both body and soul; love for the soil was an essential ingredient of patriotism. Moreover, even the greatest had no compunction in devoting some of their time to their estates, and Xenophon writes with pleasure about the care that Cyrus the Younger of Persia lavished on his 'paradise' at Sardis.

The second point to be made is this: manual labour was not, of itself, degrading. The best proof of this is that the epic heroes and their wives are often described accomplishing some practical task: Odysseus builds his own boat, Penelope spins and weaves, even Hephaestus, the divine blacksmith, spends his life in the red glow of his forge. And artists, the artisans who are inspired by the gods, are honoured and admired. In order to understand the contempt attached to manual labour two further factors must be taken into consideration: first, the ties of dependence which were created by labour, and secondly, the growth of a slave economy.

It is not the actual activity of work which makes labour despised, but the ties of dependence which it creates between the artisan and the person who uses the product which he manufactures. To build one's own house, one's own ship, or to spin and weave the material which is to clothe the members of one's own household is in no way shameful. But to work for another man, in return for a wage of any kind, is degrading. It is this which distinguishes the ancient mentality from a modern mentality which would have no hesitation in placing the independent artisan above the wage-earner. But, for the ancients, there is really no difference between the artisan who sells his own products and the workman who hires out his services. Both work to satisfy the needs of others, not their own. They depend upon others for their livelihood. For that reason they are no longer free. This is perhaps above all what distinguishes the artisan from the peasant. The peasant is so much closer to the ideal of self-sufficiency (*autarkeia*) which was the essential basis for man's freedom in the ancient world. Needless to say, in the classical age, in both Greece and Rome, this ideal of self-sufficiency had long since given way to a system of organised trade. However, the archaic mentality endured, and this explains not only the scorn felt for the artisan, labouring in his smithy, or beneath the scorching sun on the building sites, but also the scarcely veiled disdain felt for merchants or for the rich entrepreneurs who lived off the labour of their slaves. When, in fifth-century Athens, Aristophanes taxed the 'demagogues' Cleon, Hyperbolus, and Cleophon with their 'banausic' occupations, this was the feeling he was expressing, for it goes without saying that the leaders of the *demos* were not themselves manual labourers.

All the same, although the survival of an archaic mentality accounts in part for the contempt accorded to manual or mercantile occupations, it does not explain everything. The development of the institution of slavery helped to reinforce the prejudice against manual labour. It is wrong to speak, as people sometimes do, of competition between free and slave labour. Given that there was no free labour market, such competition is inconceivable. Whenever possible, free men had slaves to provide for their material needs; though, in practice, as we shall show later on, free labour always contrived to co-exist with slave labour. In Greece, at the time of the most extensive development of the slave economy, in the fifth and fourth centuries B.C., slaves and free men worked literally side by side in the fields and on public works. And the economy based on the *latifundia* system in Italy did not swallow up the small peasant who was a free man and whose praises Virgil sang. However, it became customary to allot the heaviest work to the slaves, particularly in the mines, and when the free man and the slave shared the same toil, the tendency was for them both to incur the same contempt. It is significant that the glorification of labour (in the poems of Hesiod or of Virgil and in certain writings of such Fathers of the Church as St. Basil of Caesarea) and laws against idleness (for instance those which Athenian tradition attributed to Solon) only occurred either at a time when slavery was still in its very first stages, or when it was declining, when the scarcity of labour of any kind and the rise in prices put a premium on free and individual labour, thereby creating suitable conditions for an anti-slavery ideology to develop and for a partial rehabilitation of the idea of work.

Nevertheless, even if this declared contempt for manual labour was a feature of only a limited period, and was professed only by a minority of thinkers yearning for the past, it still had profound effects upon the actual conditions of work. Even though craft guilds existed in antiquity, their object was not to protect their members. The slave revolts, when they occurred, did not have a specific programme, but at the best only expressed vague yearnings for liberty, and usually they were simply prompted by poverty and hunger. Strikes were unknown in antiquity, except in the exceptional instance of the flight of Egyptian peasants, and then the determining factor was dissatisfaction at the heavy taxes and military obligations, rather than any desire to improve working conditions. Perhaps the strangest example of all workers' revolts was the uprising of the Jewish peasants of the orator Libanius of Antioch in the fourth century A.D. Libanius said in effect that his peasants claimed the right to discuss freely with him the conditions of their employment, and he was exceedingly annoyed by such temerity. This is practically the only example in the entire history of ancient societies of a workers' revolt based upon specific claims. And even here we should not over-estimate its significance, as it occurred very late when the values of the ancient world had been severely undermined, and in an untypical region where the village communities had preserved some degree of autonomy. Was the fact that manual labour was despised also responsible for the stagnation of techniques in antiquity? It is this aspect of the general conditions of labour which we must now examine.

3
Technical Conditions

IT is not always easy to form a clear idea of ancient technology. Excavations have brought to light various utensils which it has been possible to study. Reliefs on tombstones and painted vases sometimes take as their subjects scenes from everyday life, but it is not always easy to interpret them. Then there are the writings of the ancients themselves, but descriptions of work are not very frequent. Labour on the land is the exception since it was considered more noble and treatises were devoted to agriculture. The work of the artisan did not have the same practical value, even if it was sometimes used as a paradigm in Plato's thought, and we must be thankful that Polybius and Diodorus devoted even a few lines to the miners of Spain or Egypt.

Our evidence, then, is very slight; plenty of points remain obscure, and widely differing theories have been constructed about them. However, if we restrict ourselves to general observations, two facts immediately become clear: first, the extremely primitive nature of technology in antiquity, where the use of any motive power other than animal or human was exceptional; secondly, the fact that this primitive technology persisted in the world of the city-states, so that we are left with the impression that between the eighth century B.C. and the fourth century A.D. very little progress was made, with the exception of the specialised field of military techniques which seldom had any impact on other branches of technology.

1. AGRICULTURE

The science of agronomy first appears fairly late on in the ancient world. According to Columella, a Latin

31

writer on agriculture, it was the philosopher Democritus of Abdera who first produced a treatise on the subject in the fifth century B.C. Before him, Hesiod of Boeotia had celebrated work on the land in his poem *Works and Days*, but this cannot really be considered as a technical study of agriculture. The first extant work explicitly aiming to teach the art of agriculture was Xenophon's *Oeconomicus*, and even this is written in the form of a Socratic dialogue in which technical discussions take up a relatively small part of the treatise. This was followed by the two treatises of Aristotle's pupil, Theophrastus, *History of Plants*[1] and *Causes of Plants*, and then by the many collections of the Hellenistic era, of which hardly anything remains except the mediocre *Geoponica*. In Rome, Cato was the first to introduce scientific agronomy, inspired possibly by the famous *Treatise on Agriculture* of the Carthaginian Mago, which was translated into Latin after Rome's victory in the two Punic Wars of the third century B.C. Cato's *De Agricultura* marks an important turning-point in the development of Italian agriculture. Following him, Varro (first century B.C.), Columella (first century A.D.) and Palladius (the beginning of the fifth century A.D.) completed the group of Latin writers on agriculture, while Augustus' desire to encourage a return to the land provided themes for such official poetry as Virgil's *Georgics*. Finally, Pliny's *Natural History* is invaluable, for although agriculture as such is not its subject, the book is none the less an inexhaustible mine of information.

There are of course differences between these authors, but these are more indicative of changes in the organisation of agriculture, and even in the social and political conditions of each period, than of a real evolution in technology. In fact techniques appear to have changed very little, so that a comparison of the various sources allows us to form a picture which can be assumed to

---

[1] The word *history* is here used in the old sense found in the phrase *natural history*, that is, in the sense of *inquiry*.

apply to agricultural technology in the Mediterranean throughout classical antiquity, even though account must be taken of minor differences.

Grain cultivation was clearly most important. While it was not a defining characteristic of Mediterranean agriculture, it was the basis of the daily diet, and although Athens during the Classical period (c.500–323 B.C.) and Rome from the second century B.C. onwards had to import wheat, domestic grain cultivation was still of fundamental importance. Moreover, we know that in Italy during the last few centuries of the Empire grain cultivation was gradually to replace the cultivation of vines and olives, and all the governments of antiquity attempted to encourage it.

A two-year cycle of crops seems to have been the rule in the ancient world. A three-year cycle was only seldom practised, and at a late date. And even if the ancients were aware of the principle of crop rotation, it remained a general rule until the end of antiquity that land lay fallow one year in two, or one year in three. The fallow period was primarily designed to allow the land to recover after an exhausting harvest. Moreover, allowing the land to lie fallow every other year enabled the soil to store up humidity. Spacing out the harvests compensated for the insufficiency of the rainy seasons of the Mediterranean where the rains are heavy but short-lived.

The first ploughing took place in the spring. We know from illustrations (*for example, see Plate* Ia) the type of plough used; it was a simple wooden swing-plough, pointed, either with or without a metal ploughshare, and unable to dig deeply into the earth, which suited the thin and stony soils of the Mediterranean countries. In the *Georgics* (I, 169–175) Virgil gives a poetic description of this swing-plough which has given rise to many tricky problems of translation and interpretation:

> . . . the forest elm is bowed by main force to bend into a share-beam, and takes the shape of the curving plough; to the stock of it are fitted the long eight-foot pole, the two

mould-boards, and the double back of the share-head; and
the light lime is cut to season for the yoke, and the tall
beech for the plough tail that is to turn the carriage from
above and behind . . .

In Hesiod, the beam is made of holm oak, the pole of
bay and elm, the stock or sole of oak, but the general
shape of the instrument and the elements which compose
it are still the same eight centuries later, although the
swing-plough made in one piece, the *autogyon* which
Hesiod recommended to be used as an alternative to
the composite plough, seems to have disappeared quite
early on. Such an elementary instrument would demand
a great effort from the man using it: the ploughman had
not only to exert pressure with his hand, but also, as can
be seen in many illustrations, to push on the protruding
piece of the stock with his foot. The plough was usually
drawn by two animals, oxen or mules, but Pliny mentions yokes of two or three pairs of oxen (*Natural History*
XVIII, 48).

The work of the plough had often to be completed by
hand. Hesiod (*Works and Days*, 469–471) recommended
the ploughman to have following behind him a slave
with a mattock, who would 'make trouble for the birds
by hiding the seed', and Aristophanes mentions among
the instruments which could not legally be pawned the
sphyra, a sort of mallet to break up the clods of earth.
The harrow was also used for this purpose.

The aim of the preliminary ploughing was to bury the
weeds which would decompose and make fertiliser, and
to allow the soil to be permeated by the welcome rain. A
second ploughing took place in the summer. It was supposed to 'allow the land to be baked by the sun' (Xenophon, *Oeconomicus*, XVI, 14). There was often a third
or even a fourth ploughing in the autumn, immediately
before the sowing which Theophrastus puts 'at the
setting of the Pleiades', that is, at the beginning of Nov-
ember. However, this was not an absolute rule, and
Ischomachus, one of the 'speakers' in the *Oeconomicus*,

suggests that the sowing should be spread out over the entire season in order to assure a more or less constant harvest regardless of whether the first rains come early or late.

The sowing was not the last of the preliminary agricultural operations: during the winter the farmer had to make sure to pull up the weeds which could smother the plants, and he had to fork the earth in order to free the young shoots from the new layer of soil which covered them after the rains; and the soil had to be ridged when the roots were laid bare.

The harvest was reaped at the beginning of the summer. A small scythe was used, and the work was always done by hand. It is doubtful whether Pliny's famous and controversial reaper was ever used. Once cut, the wheat was threshed and winnowed. Threshing was carried out by domestic animals, oxen, mules or goats, which trampled on the ears of grain. In Hesiod's day, however, slaves were still harnessed to this task. Next, the wheat was winnowed. Xenophon gives a precise description of the winnowing operation in the *Oeconomicus* (XVIII, 6–8): the threshed wheat was tossed into the air with a spade or a winnowing basket; the light straw was borne away on the wind, and only the grain fell back on to the threshing floor. It was then measured and stored in barns.

We have very much less information about techniques for cultivating vines and olive trees, although arboriculture held a prominent place in ancient Mediterranean agriculture. Xenophon's *Oeconomicus* devotes three chapters to grain cultivation compared to only one on arboriculture. On the other hand, the Latin writers give a wealth of detail on the method of planting a vine: the first operation was the deep digging, to rid the soil of all the vegetation which had overrun it and all the roots of other plants which could poison it. This deep digging was carried out the year before the vine was planted, during the winter and the spring. The most widespread technique was to dig ditches to a depth of

D

between one-and-a-half and two-and-a-half feet in Greece, and between two-and-a-half and four feet in Italy, with a width of probably about two feet in both cases. (Nowadays, the depth of the ditches is about six feet around Rome, four-and-a-half feet in Portugal, and nearly one-and-a-half feet in the Beaujolais district and in Burgundy.)

The best ground for planting vines was dry and well exposed to the sun, in other words, chalky hills. The vine was planted preferably in spring or in autumn. The ancient authors generally agree about the way the young vine was planted. First of all, the upper cutting of the seedling was trimmed, all the vine shoots except one were cut back, and most of the radicles were removed. To plant the seedlings, they started by laying them out along the middle of the trench, then they trained them up against the sides in the shape of a reversed gamma, so that two buds showed above the ground. They were covered with a little earth and with a bed of pebbles and shells. They were fertilised with manure, and then the trench was filled up with earth which was packed down under foot. Finally the earth was heaped up round the shoot as a precaution against desiccation.

Vines were rarely cultivated on their own. Most frequently the vines were separated by fruit trees or grew amid fields of beans or barley. The vine needed meticulous care. It was often provided with a support, usually some tree: elm, black poplar, ash, fig tree, olive tree, or sometimes a vine prop about three feet high. For the grapes to ripen well, any leaves covering them had to be removed, and the bunches of grapes had to be picked as they ripened so that those that were still green could develop better. The pruning consisted in snipping off the ends of the shoots to concentrate the sap in the bunches of grapes and in the main stem. Sometimes too, a thin band of bark was removed just above the bunches in order to stop the sap rising and to allow time for the pollination to be completed.

The grape harvests usually took place in mid-September, lasting till the end of October. This required the use of a seasonal labour force which also took part in the wine-making.

There are very few sources of information about the cultivation of the olive. The olive trees were either planted along the sides of roads, or in the middle of fields, in quincunxes. According to Columella it was possible to plant 160 olive trees to every five acres. The seedlings were placed in fairly deep holes and the shoots were held up by logs. To avoid them drying up or rotting, the tips of all the seedlings were covered with clay. In the *Georgics*, Virgil emphasises how little care olive trees need. But in fact, just as for the vines, the roots had to be laid bare in the spring, and the seedlings earthed up in the autumn. Columella (V, 9) is also emphatic about the use of pruning. He sums up the essentials of olive cultivation succinctly: 'He who ploughs the olive-grove asks it for fruit, he who manures it begs for fruit, he who lops it forces it to yield fruit.' The green olives were gathered in the autumn, the black in December; the latter gave the better oil.

Clearly all this required no complicated apprenticeship. Agronomy was more of a moral system than a *techne*, and for this reason work in the fields was regarded by the ancients as a kind of school for virtue and courage. The earth was just and gave her fruits to those who understood how to tend her, and who obeyed the injunctions of the gods. Whatever magical practices they resorted to, in order to obtain good harvests, they certainly never took the place of the day-to-day care the earth needed, and experience was the basis of this knowledge which was handed down from father to son. But the science of agriculture went no further than an attempt to find better ways of organising labour. Whatever technical progress took place in agriculture depended on particular social and political conditions which favoured the development of the large, or rather fairly large, property within which it was possible to organise the different agricultural operations on a more

37

rational basis. This was the aim of Xenophon's *Oeco-nomicus*, which had the landowner, Ischomachus, declaring that agriculture is easy to learn, and which attempted to describe the best way of organising labour on a fairly large farm. This was also the purpose of Cato's *De Agricultura*, and of the treatises of Varro and Columella. It is interesting to note that they all describe the type of estate which appears to be characteristic of the ancient city, covering sixty to seventy-five acres, sufficiently large to make possible a rational division of labour, but small enough for the master or overseer to direct the labour personally. It is only with this context and when conditions such as these prevailed that we can speak of improvements in agricultural techniques in antiquity.

2. MANUFACTURE

If we are fairly well informed about agricultural techniques in antiquity, this is far from being the case with industrial work. Ancient authors were seldom concerned with the methods of work of the artisans, and it is chiefly by studying the products of their work and from the rare illustrations that we can form some idea of the techniques of ancient manufacture.

The manufacture of textiles must be considered separately. In an ancient city this was usually the concern of the women of the household, and only in rare cases did it reach the stage of artisan manufacture in the strict sense of the term. And even then, spinning and weaving were still reserved for female workers and the technique was completely elementary. Only the operations of fulling or dyeing involved more complex equipment and were undertaken by a generally more specialised labour force. Briefly, industrial labour, as such, concerned three essential fields: pottery, metallurgy and the working of wood and stone.

Pottery is one of the most ancient crafts of all, and potters, together with smith and carpenters, were the

Ia

Ib

Ia Ploughman in an olive orchard: Roman mosaic from Cherchel in Algeria

Ib Cherubs as goldsmiths: wall painting from the House of the Vettii, Pompeii

II Shoemaker's shop: Attic black-figured vase, *c.* 500 B.C.

first artisans in the villages of antiquity. Decorated vases were produced in all areas of the Greek world. The Geometric style, which predominated during the Greek Dark Age, was to be found in Attica as well as in the Peloponnese, central Greece and the islands. The Orientalizing style which succeeded it flourished particularly in Ionia and in the Aegean islands, and was at its peak in Corinth during the seventh century B.C. and the beginning of the sixth. From the sixth century B.C. onwards Attic pottery dominated in the Aegean world, and a narrative decorative style became established. Thanks to ancient authors and also to vase-paintings, we are quite well informed about the techniques of the manufacture of Greek vases, especially about Athenian ceramics. Moreover, because pottery can also provide the best means for dating sites, archaeologists have for many years attempted to determine its characteristics with a high degree of precision. These studies have made it possible to appreciate with what care the clay used for making the vases was chosen: in Attica, the clay most used came from Cape Colias to the south-west of the city of Athens, and it was mixed with *miltos*, or red ochre, which had the effect of making it less porous. The vase was made on the wheel, then dried in the open air before being painted or incised.

In Attica, to start with, black silhouettes were painted on the red background of the clay, and then, from late in the sixth century onwards, it was the background which was given a shiny black glaze while the figures appeared in red, which allowed the craftsman more subtlety in his design. Towards the middle of the fifth century B.C., red-figure painting became more complex and richer, with other colours being added, especially blues, pinks and some warm shades of brown.

Once decorated, the vases were placed in the kiln. It has been estimated that they were fired at a temperature between 900° and 950°C, which is of course very much lower than the temperatures reached in modern kilns. For this reason these vases were rather fragile since the clay remained brittle. Many vases must have been broken during the firing. The glazing operation, which gave the vases the splendid lustre which we can still admire, took place after the firing and was supposed to correct any imperfections caused by it.

Painted vases disappeared almost completely at the end of the fourth century B.C., and from the beginning of the Hellenistic period pottery began to be produced on which the relief decoration was inspired by that of metal objects. The first to appear were the famous 'Megarian bowls', which were in fact produced throughout the eastern basin of the Mediterranean, then came the Arretine pottery of Italy, which reached its peak in the first century A.D., and finally the 'sigillated' Gallo-Roman pottery. At this stage, the vases were no longer thrown on the wheel, but moulded, which is a far more industrialised technique but entails a definite drop in the artistic quality. However, one fact remained constant throughout antiquity: whether they were thrown or moulded, ceramic wares could be made with very simple equipment. So, even in the Roman period, although production was sometimes concentrated geographically, as is shown by the distribution of kilns, it never developed into large industrial units but remained in the hands of the small craftsmen. Moreover, even when within a single workshop labour was divided between workers, each responsible for different tasks, this was done mostly for the sake of convenience and was not organised systematically.

The same could be said for metallurgy. It was a basic industry as it provided men with the tools used in everyday life, and above all with arms. The ancients had achieved great skill in this domain at an early date. Although Homer's description of the making of Achilles' shield by Hephaestus is of course poetic rather than technical, we know from surviving examples what masterpieces the Greek bronze-workers were able to produce. In Athens, as late as the fourth century B.C., certain craftsmen were renowned for the quality of the

arms which came from their workshops, and in the pre-
vious century the wealth of the armourer Cephalus,
father of the orator Lysias, was well known: when in 404,
the Thirty, who were the rulers of Athens, seized the
workshop he had bequeathed to his sons, they took 700
shields, a large quantity of gold, silver, jewels and furni-
ture, and 120 slaves (Lysias, *Against Erathosthenes*, 19).
By the late Roman period, metallurgy had become an
industry controlled for the most part by the state which
itself owned mines and workshops. But there had been
little evolution in techniques.

The basic problem was to obtain sufficiently high
temperatures for the reduction of the ore. Now, in
general the ancients knew of only one type of fuel—
wood, or rather charcoal. Ancient authors—in particular
Theophrastus in his *History of Plants* and Pliny in his
Natural History—discuss at length the relative merits of
various substances as fuel. Theophrastus recommends
oak and, in general, young trees; Pliny recommends
conifers. In the Roman period charcoal was exported to
other parts of the Roman world from places where it was
produced, such as southern Italy, Macedonia, the region
around Mount Ida in Crete, and Gaul; and records of
prices from Delos give us information about the nature
and organisation of this trade. It should be added that
they did not altogether ignore other fuels such as
graphite, asphalt, lignite, coal and peat.

Another problem was ventilation. We know of various
types of bellows. Homer mentions the *askos* or leather
bellows, a kind of leather bottle which can be seen in
many later vase-paintings. The word *physa* in Greek and
follis in Latin are other terms to describe the blacksmith's bellows, but they appear to cover a more or less
similar type of bellows which underwent very few modi-
fications right up to the end of the classical age.

As for the furnaces themselves, it has been possible to
make a study of the remains of ancient furnaces actually
used for smelting ore and fusing metals. The more
advanced were of the type known as 'shaft-furnaces', in

which the ore or the metal was heated together with the fuel. Often these furnaces could be employed only once, as they were made unusable by the deposits of corrosive substances. This explains why there are so many furnaces on one site. However, when the furnace, or at least its interior, was made of stone, it lasted longer. The stone which lined the inner walls of the oven was selected very carefully according to the type of ore to be used. The older type of furnace also remained in use for a long time and was still to be found in the Roman period. As a rule it consisted simply of a hole dug in the ground, lined with clay; in the Roman period two holes were sometimes dug side by side, joined by a chimney. It was also possible to smelt metal in large earthenware vessels (*pithoi* in Greek), the purpose of which was to keep the metal in an easily adaptable form. At any rate, that is what would seem to be suggested by a rather curious passage of Herodotus (III, 96): 'The tribute is stored by the king [of Persia] in this fashion: he melts it down and pours it into earthen vessels; when the vessel is full he breaks the earthenware away, and when he needs money coins as much as will serve his purpose.' It seems likely that in Roman times such clay receptacles were frequently placed inside the furnace in order to keep the iron ore separate from the fuel. They were particularly necessary in the making of steel.

All this was still fairly primitive, as were the tools of the smith: hammers, pliers, forceps and so on. Metal was sometimes worked into articles of a quite remarkable quality, and yet this work was still done essentially by hand. The technique of welding was for a long time most elementary: pieces of metal were assembled by rivets or nails. Welding by fusion did not make its appearance until fairly late. One of the most famous examples was the Colossus of Rhodes, constructed in the third century B.C. The Romans used a similar technique in making lead pipes for their aqueducts.

The techniques of metallurgy were thus closer to those of an artist than those of an artisan. This was also true of stone-work. It is here perhaps that we can get the clearest idea of ancient technology as there is evidence from inscriptions[1] as well as from archaeology, and above all because we possess the remarkable theoretical work of the architect and engineer Vitruvius, written in Latin in the first century A.D.

To begin with, we have detailed information about the equipment of stone workers: the saw, the hammer, the cutting tools and the drill, and besides these a series of different tools which were used to finish off the cutting of the stone, for redressing the walls, for polishing, chiselling, sculpting mouldings and so on. It is not possible to describe all the tools mentioned in the texts, which cover a wide range and reveal the extreme precision and diversity of the operations. One passage from a distinguished contemporary authority on ancient architecture will serve to illustrate:

A certain number of tools were common to both (the sculptor and the mason) and were borrowed from the equipment of the sculptor, such as the fine narrow chisel, sometimes with rounded ends for outlining contours (arches for instance) or the gouge for picking out rowels or the interlacing decoration at the base of Ionic columns. Specifications from Lebadea describe the kind of cutting blade used for the different types of redressing. The surface of joints or layers at the anathyroses were to be thinned down with a coarse serrated cutter, the bush hammer of modern stone-masons. The redressing of the centre of the surface of marble slabs would be done with a simple serrated blade. The bands around the edge, which were the guide areas for the final redressing, were worked with a gradine (a serrated chisel with close-set pointed teeth). The preparation of the anathyroses (the surfaces of contact of the joints) was carried out with a flat chisel. Finally, the main lines of the finest chiselling and the engraving of the inscriptions were carried out with a chasing chisel or a chisel with an extremely narrow blade.

[1] See Appendix I.

(Roland Martin, *Manuel d'architecture grecque*, vol. I (Paris, 1965), p. 183, omitting the Greek terms which he quotes). The 'specifications from Lebadea', on which the passage is based, appear in a long inscription from that small Boetian city laying down in minute detail the specifications for a temple under construction.

From this description we can see how a single type of tool, the chisel, could be adapted to different operations in the cutting and sculpting of stone. The same could be said for other tools, the trepan, the drill, the set-square, the ruler and the compass, on which we possess textual or pictorial evidence.

Some of the operations, such as polishing, redressing, chiselling and sculpting, were undertaken after the stones had been laid. The latter operation involved the use of various techniques and sometimes genuine machinery. Pliny (*Natural History* XXXVI, 19) gives us a description of the technique used for placing the coping of the Parthenon: 'The architect in charge of the work was Chersiphron. The crowning marvel was his success in lifting the architraves of this massive building into place. This he achieved by filling bags of plaited reed with sand and constructing a gently graded ramp which reached the upper surfaces of the capitals of the columns. Then, little by little, he emptied the lowest layer of bags, so that the fabric gradually settled into its right position.' However, inscriptions show that even in the fifth century B.C. lifting machinery was used, operated by the derrick, the winch and the pulley and tackle, and Vitruvius, the great Roman architect, has left us detailed descriptions of these machines.

Although such machines increased the energy generated by human labour, they did not replace it. Only exceptional problems prompted men to develop exceptional techniques. The engineers of antiquity were aware of the power of water, but they very seldom made use of it, and anyway not until a relatively late date. The stagnation of technology in the ancient world therefore cannot be explained, as has sometimes been suggested, by the *inability* of the ancients to perfect it. Ancient science, particularly during the Hellenistic period, reached a very high level of abstract reasoning and also produced a few remarkable practical applications. The reason these inventions were never applied to the techniques of work, except in a few limited fields, was that the prevailing social, political and ideological conditions did nothing to stimulate such an application.

Primitive techniques developed very little in the course of whole centuries in the history of Greek and Roman antiquity. The political and social system created values according to which work for the benefit of another was considered a form of servitude, and an obstacle to the free development of the 'political animal', the citizen. Objectively, among the most important conditions were the existence of personal slavery, and the enslavement of cities or of subject peoples, so that minorities could enjoy a state of idleness which eventually turned them into parasites. These were the conditions affecting work in the world of the city-states of antiquity, and above all in Greece and Rome.

PART TWO

SMALLHOLDERS AND LARGE
LANDOWNERS

4
Smallholders

THE essential basis for the ancient city was, we have seen, a community of small farmers who were free and who owned their land. Although the historical evolution of the Greek cities and of Rome soon changed this original social structure, nevertheless the citizen-soldier who owned his land remained the social ideal for antiquity. We can form a fairly clear idea of his life, his interests and his problems, for he became a common literary theme and the hero *par excellence* in particular of Attic comedy, which provides us with a somewhat conventional but still quite lively picture of the Greek peasant. Down the ages, the Boeotian peasant of Hesiod corresponds to Aristophanes' Athenian peasant and to the Roman peasant in the Republican tradition and in Virgil.

This peasant was first and foremost a citizen. In fact it was often because he owned a small parcel of land that he qualified to be one, and this was what distinguished him in Athens from those *thetes* who owned nothing and in Rome from the *proletarii* who lived from hand to mouth. It is important to remember that to own land was a privilege reserved exclusively for the members of the civic community, and that, however rich they may have been, foreigners were not allowed to buy even a small parcel of land belonging to the city. As a citizen the peasant was expected to bear arms in defence of his country. In times of war he left his home and his fields, but as soon as the fighting was over, he returned to harvest his crops. That is why military campaigns seldom continued beyond the early days of summer, and it was not rare for peasants to desert if the war went on too long. The Peloponnesian War in Greece and Rome's great wars of conquest were fatal to the small peasant for this very reason. Aristophanes' *Peace* was performed in

Athens in 421 when the negotiations which were to lead to the peace of Nicias were just getting under way. It shows how anxious the peasants were to get back to their calm pastoral life, and how idyllic that life appeared to them.

All the same, considered more closely, the life of the small peasant in Italy or in Greece was not an easy one, especially in Greece where the soil was poor, and in the mountain districts the climate was harsh. A man had to rise early and often work through the day under a blistering sun if he hoped to make a livelihood from a poor soil. As Hesiod says (*Works and Days*, 391–395) to his brother Perses:

> Strip to sow and strip to plough and strip to reap, if you wish to get in all Demeter's fruits in due season, and that each kind may grow in its season. Else, afterwards, you may chance to be in want, and go begging to other men's houses, but without avail.

Laziness was indeed the greatest pitfall for the peasant. It is Hesiod too who offers the following advice (*Works and Days*, 574–578):

> Avoid shady seats and sleeping until dawn in the harvest season, when the sun scorches the body. Then be busy, and bring home your fruits, getting up early to make your livelihood sure.

He also gives this striking description of the trials of winter (*Works and Days*, 503–512):

> Avoid the month Lenaeon,[1] wretched days, all of them fit to skin an ox, and the frosts which are cruel when Boreas blows over the earth. He blows across horse-breeding Thrace upon the wide sea and stirs it up, while earth and the forest howl. On many a high-leafed oak and thick pine he falls and brings them to the bounteous earth in mountain glens: then all the immense wood roars . . .

---

[1] Lenaeon falls in late January and early February. This is the earliest reference to a month-name in Greek literature.

The peasant's house was usually no more than a hut. In winter men and beasts lived there together, and in the summer they all lived outdoors. This was the time when life could be enjoyed to the full—for the picture is not an entirely gloomy one. From Hesiod (*Works and Days*, 582–595), again, we take this description of the joys of summer:

> But when the artichoke flowers, and the chirping grass-hopper sits in a tree and pours down his shrill song continually from under his wings in the season of wearisome heat, then goats are plumpest and wine sweetest; women are most wanton, but men are feeblest, because Sirius parches head and knees and the skin is dry through heat. But at that time let me have a shady rock and wine of Byblos, a clot of curds and milk of drained goats with the flesh of a heifer fed in the woods, that has never calved, and of firstling kids; then also let me drink bright wine, sitting in the shade, when my heart is satisfied with food, and so, turning my head to face the fresh Zephyr . . .

This was the time for feasting and merriment, when the gods were honoured amid happy celebrations (Aristophanes, *Ecclesiazusae*, 838–852):

> Come, for the tables now are all prepared
> And laden heavily with all good things:
> The couches all with rugs and cushions piled!
> They're mixing wine: the perfume-selling girls
> Are ranged in order: collops on the fire:
> Hares on the spit; and in the oven, cakes;
> Chaplets are woven: comfits parched and dried.
> The youngest girls are boiling pots of broth . . .
> Come, therefore, come, and quickly: bread in hand
> The pantler stands; and open wide your mouths.

Aristophanes' plays are full of such descriptions which must have delighted the spectators. When Strepsiades, in the *Clouds*, evokes past happiness he dreams of the figs in his garden, the honey from his bees, and the smell of garlic and of thyme, as if these were part of an irretrievable paradise.

The gods were associated with these celebrations. They were inseparable from the life of the peasant, and although we are familiar with the ritual nature of the Roman peasant's religion, which survived until a fairly late date, we should also remember that Hesiod's poem aimed at establishing precisely the sacrifices and prayers which should be addressed to the gods in order to obtain a good harvest. It is interesting to compare Hesiod's advice (*Works and Days*, 336–340) with Cato's in the *De Agricultura* (141) five centuries later. It was important not only to avoid offending the gods, but also to respect their rules and to conciliate them with the appropriate sacrifices:

As far as you are able, sacrifice to the deathless gods purely and cleanly, and burn rich meats also, and at other times propitiate them with libations and incense, both when you go to bed and when the holy light has come back, so that they may be gracious to you in heart and spirit . . .

That with the good help of the gods success may crown our work, I bid thee Manius, to take care to purify my farm, my land, my ground with this *suovetaurilia* [three victims, a swine, a ram, and a bull], in whatever part thou thinkest best for them to be driven or carried around. Make a prayer with wine to Janus and Jupiter, and say: 'Father Mars, I pray and beseech thee that thou be gracious and merciful to me, my house and my household; to which intent I have bidden this *suovetaurilia* to be led around my land, my ground, my farm; that thou keep away, ward off, and remove sickness, seen and unseen, barrenness and destruction, ruin and unseasonable influence; and that thou permit my harvests, my grain, my vineyards, and my plantations to flourish and to come to good issue, preserve in health my shepherds and my flocks, and give good health and strength to me, my house, and my household . . .

SMALLHOLDERS

The utilitarian purpose of these prayers was so obvious that when, in Aristophanes' comedy, the *Plutus*, the poet restores sight to the god of riches, Hermes comes to complain in the name of the gods that since poverty has disappeared (1113–1116):

> No laurel, meal-cake, victim, frankincense,
> Has any man on any altar laid
> Or aught beside.

Of course, the poet was joking, and we may be sure that those who laughed at the discomfiture of Hermes were nevertheless careful, on their return home, to accomplish scrupulously any rites which might be expected to conciliate the gods. We also know how important the agrarian festivals were in ancient religion. In Athens, Demeter, the goddess who had presented mankind with wheat, and Dionysus, the god of wine, were particularly venerated, and it was customary to offer to the gods the first fruits of the harvest. In Rome most of the festivals were associated with important moments in the rural calendar, and, like the Greek gods, the Roman gods were or had been gods of plenty or protective gods who warded off evil and bad weather. The deeply rural character of ancient religion, which endured throughout the classical age, shows how important the role of the peasant was in the cities of antiquity.

To assess the importance of this peasant population in the economic life of the ancient cities, we shall have to consider the Greek peasant and the Roman peasant separately, as the problems were different and their evolution was not equally rapid.

When we speak of the Greek peasant we usually think of Athens, although small-scale farming was not restricted to Attica. The many references we have made to Hesiod show that it was also a feature in Boeotia, and the evidence from inscriptions indicates that it was to be found in the islands and in some parts of the Peloponnese. However, it is only for Attica that we possess enough information to reach fairly definite conclusions.

It is in Athens in the fifth and fourth centuries B.C. that we can best assess the place held by the peasant in the economy of the city.

It is difficult to make definite calculations either for the acreage of the farms or for the approximate yield of the land. There are not enough precise data and it is therefore impossible to construct a proper time-series. But still, it is indicative that a gift of 200 plethra of land (about forty acres), made by the Athenian state to the grandson of Aristides at the end of the fifth century, was considered very generous by Demosthenes, and the largest known estate in Attica, belonging to Phaenippus and estimated to be about 740 acres, certainly appears to have been exceptional.[1] An estate could of course be divided into various units, and would comprise farms from several different districts in Attica. But the fact is that small estates of less than twenty-five acres were the general rule, and these small estates were often farmed by the owner in person. Tenant farming seems not to have been wide-spread in Athens in the Classical period, except on land belonging to temples or in the case of land belonging to children which was let out for them by their guardians.

These small farms were seldom devoted to a single crop. The evidence from legal speeches reinforces the impression given by the comedies: the peasant of Athens did cultivate some cereals, but seldom on a scale large enough for his needs. Chremes, in the *Ecclesiazusae*, sells his grapes in order to buy flour. Since Solon's day the cultivation of vineyards and olive groves had gradually taken the place of grain farming, which was hard work and not very profitable. The peasant of Attica was really a vine-grower and a gardener rather than a farmer. For this reason the ideal of self-sufficiency was no more than

[1] This estimate which is accepted by most modern critics has recently been challenged by G. E. M. de Ste. Croix in 'The Estate of Phaenippus', in *Studies presented to Victor Ehrenberg*, pp. 109 *ff*, where the area of Phaenippus' estate is calculated to be about 100 acres, or forty hectares.

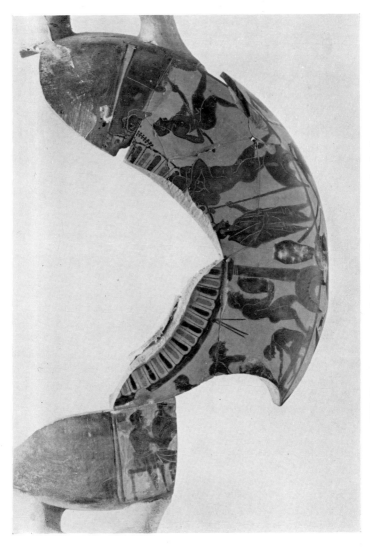

III Potters at work: late 6th century Attic jug

IV Ironmonger: terracotta relief on tomb,
Isola Sacra, Ostia, 1st century A.D.

a distant memory. Naturally, the farmers attempted to live off their land as far as possible. They grew a little wheat, owned a few olive trees, a few fig trees, and a few lovingly tended vines. They reared a few pigs, chickens, perhaps some bees, a goat who gave them milk and cheese, and sometimes, if they were rich, some sheep and a pair of oxen or mules. If there were any surplus products these were sold in the market. The peasant himself seldom went to market; he sent his wife or a slave. Thus, Euripides' mother sold greenstuff in the market, and Aristophanes pokes fun at this.

The agricultural produce of these little farms did not, of course, hold a place of much importance in the revenues of Athens. The money from the surplus produce sold in the market made it possible to buy a little flour, maybe a few tools, some ordinary pots, or a pair of shoes. Clothes though were generally made at home by the peasant's wife, who was sometimes helped by a young servant. Although Attica was able to export oil and wine, it is unlikely that the small peasants profited, and there cannot have been many coins accumulated in strong-boxes at home; they were needed at the busiest seasons of the year to pay the wages of a temporary farm labourer, or on occasion to buy a slave or a mule. Aristophanes' comedies often take as heroes the *autourgoi*, the men who cultivated their own land, and show us that most of them had at least one slave, if not more, despite the small size of their property and a life which was often hard. The slave helped his master in the fields and also acted as servant. Chremylus, who complains of being poor, nevertheless had a slave, or even several slaves, and not to possess a single slave was a sign of extreme poverty. These slaves performed all the hardest tasks. But in everyday life they shared the meals of their masters, and the freedom with which they expressed themselves in the comedies indicates the degree to which they were integrated in the life of the household. When the busiest times of year came round, the farmer might hire the services of an agricultural labourer, one of the free men with no possessions whom poverty forced to work on other men's land. But as one can imagine, more often he borrowed the slave or slaves of a neighbour, on an exchange basis. Naturally, amicable relationships were necessary for such an arrangement. The legal speeches provide information about the disputes which sometimes arose between two neighbouring landowners, with one accusing the other of diverting the water to his own advantage or of trespassing without good reason upon land which did not belong to him. Generally, however, peasants belonging to the same deme (parish) met at the deme assemblies which they attended much more willingly than the meetings of the city assembly where they felt rather lost and at a disadvantage among the townsfolk. The deme formed a living community, with its own religious ceremonies, its own meetings, its country festivals. It was the very kernel of Athenian democracy.

The Peloponnesian War dealt a severe blow to this class of small farmers. Since the exigencies of the war which he was determined to wage obliged Pericles to bring the peasants inside the walls of Athens, they had to abandon their fields. Thucydides describes their deplorable condition, which made it possible for the plague to spread so quickly, and Aristophanes echoes their laments and their regrets. After the war many of them did not return to the devastated countryside. In order to recultivate a vineyard or an olive grove one had to be able to live for several years without the least hope of a harvest. Very few were in a position to do this. The last two comedies of Aristophanes, the *Ecclesiazusae* and the *Plutus*, give a graphic picture of the terrible poverty of the Athenian peasant at the beginning of the fourth century. Praxagora, describing her 'communist' programme, justifies it by saying (*Ecclesiazusae*, 590–593):

The rule which I dare to enact and declare
Is that all shall be equal, and equally share
All wealth and enjoyments, nor longer endure

That one should be rich, and another be poor,
That one should have acres, far-stretching and wide,
And another not even enough to provide
Himself with a grave: that this at his call
Should have hundreds of servants, and that none at all.

And Chremylus, addressing Poverty, tells her what she
has given to the peasants of Attica (*Plutus*, 542–546):

For a robe but a rag, for a bed but a bag of rushes which
    harbour a nation
Of bugs whose envenomed and tireless attacks would the
    soundest of sleepers awaken.
And then for a carpet a sodden old mat, which is falling
    to bits, must be taken.
And a jolly hard stone for a pillow you'll own; and for
    girdle cakes barley and wheaten,
Must leaves dry and lean of the radish or e'en sour stalks
    of the mallow be eaten.
And the head of a barrel, stove in, for a chair; and instead
    of a trough for your kneading
A stave of a vat you must borrow, and that all broken . . .

Of course, we must allow for exaggeration in a
comedy. In the fourth century the land was still divided
among many people and there were still considerable
numbers of landowners. All the same, the laments of
political writers and philosophers over the disappearance
of the class of free small farmers foreshadow, at a distance
of two centuries, the reflections of Tiberius Gracchus
when faced with the abandoned Italian countryside.

Unfortunately, the life of the Roman peasant is not
nearly so well documented as that of the Greek, as
recorded by Hesiod and Aristophanes. There are only
the writers of the Augustan era, who, to serve the
political ends of their prince, produced a reconstruction
of the traditional role of the Roman peasant. Agriculture
does indeed seem to have been, from the earliest times,
the essential occupation of the people of Latium. Cereals,
vines and olives, the traditional crops of Mediterranean

countries, were cultivated there by methods which, as we have said, differed hardly at all from those used by the Greek peasant. At about the time when the laws known as the Twelve Tables were drawn up, towards the middle of the fifth century B.C., the small estate was definitely predominant, and the old style Roman cultivating his own fields and only leaving them in order to serve his country is typified by the famous example of Cincinnatus.

From the fourth century onwards things began to change: the early conquests in Italy considerably extended the land which was still state property, the *ager publicus*. This land belonged to everyone. The state gave permission to use it to anyone who applied to do so, on payment of a *vectigal*. The wealthiest people managed to occupy increasingly large portions of the *ager publicus*, and their *occupatio* was gradually transformed into virtual possession. To start with this did not make much difference to the Italian agricultural countryside or to the structure of rural society. The few large landowners left the cultivation of their newly acquired land to poor peasants who thus became their clients. Small-scale farming therefore remained the rule and the peasant farmer, by whatever right he occupied the land, worked his fields with the help of one or two slaves, seldom more. When he went to town it was to vote for his patron, and not to try to influence the politics of the city, as Aristophanes' peasant did. He also went to town to take to the weekly market the surplus from his garden—a few vegetables or a little flour which he exchanged for a few of those heavy bronze coins which were probably not minted before the middle of the fourth century.

However, the wars of conquest were to bring profound changes to the situation of the Roman peasant. In the first place, his protracted absence from his land during the long years of war had similar consequences to those in Greece at the time of the Peloponnesian War. The peasant who returned to his land which had been abandoned for several years very often preferred to sell up rather than attempt to recultivate it. Everything combined to encourage such a decision, for instance, the general drop in the price of corn, following the influx of grain from Sicily and North Africa which was having the effect of turning Italian landowners to the more lucrative culture of vines and olives, or to stock-raising. As we have already observed, considerable capital is necessary for arboriculture. Despite the plunder which he had brought back from the wars, the small peasant did not usually have sufficient funds for such an outlay. And he was all the more tempted to sell up since the price of land had risen because of the influx of capital following the great conquests. This accounts for the rapid concentration of the land, and the transformation of much agricultural land into pasture-land, while the employment of slave labour became increasingly general.

The peasant had only two alternatives: to swell the ranks of the urban population in Rome, or to work as an agricultural labourer on land belonging to someone else. We know from Cato's *De Agricultura* how wretched was the position of these *politores*, sharecroppers of a sort, who received a portion of the farm produce in return for cultivating the land: at the harvest they received only a minute proportion of the yield, one-ninth on rich farmland, one-sixth on poor soil. Nevertheless, they had a better lot than that of the hired agricultural labourers, the *mercenarii* who lived in constant fear of unemployment. They were faced with the competition of slave labour. For, all those slaves thrown onto the Italian markets by the wars of conquest provided a labour force which was not only more profitable, but also often better qualified for the specialised cultures.

We know how far-reaching were the consequences of the agrarian crisis in Italy towards the middle of the second century B.C., and what efforts were made by certain reformers to re-establish that class of peasants which had provided the foundation for the greatness of the

59

Roman Republic. It is interesting, too, to detect an echo of the words of Praxagora in the famous speech which Plutarch (*Tiberius Gracchus*, 9) puts into the mouth of Tiberius Gracchus:

> The wild beasts that roam over Italy [he would say], have every one of them a cave or lair to lurk in; but the men who fight and die for Italy enjoy the common air and light, indeed, but nothing else; houseless and homeless they wander about with their wives and children. And it is with lying lips that their imperators exhort the soldiers in their battles to defend sepulchres and shrines from the enemy; for not a man of them has an hereditary altar, not one of all these many Romans an ancestral tomb, but they fight and die to support others in wealth and luxury, and though they are styled masters of the world, they have not a single clod of earth that is their own.

However, we know too what obstacles confronted Tiberius and later Caius Gracchus when they attempted in vain to recover public land which had been illegally occupied. Their policy of redividing it into small allotments failed. Or rather, it took a different form from that intended. The colonies of veterans, which were going to be further increased by the generals of the first century, brought into being in Italy itself, and even more in the provinces, a new social type: the smallholder who had been a soldier. He owned a medium-sized property which he could afford to cultivate under favourable conditions since his share of booty enabled him to acquire a slave labour force which he controlled very strictly.

But can he still be called a peasant? In Italy, at the end of the Republic and at the beginning of the Empire, the self-sufficient cultivator living off his small-holding no longer existed. It was only towards the middle of the second century A.D., when the grave agrarian crisis which was to bring about the downfall of the Empire was beginning to be felt, that extensive cereal cultivation and small-scale farming reappeared in Italy. But it did so in an entirely different social context: the small cultivator who held a long lease of the land, legally a *colonus*, was on the road which finally led to a form of personal serfdom.

It is not within the scope of this work to discuss at any length the problem of the 'colonate', which tended to become the basis for social relationships in the countryside in the late Empire, at least in the western part of the Empire. It is worth noting that this type of tenancy first made its appearance in Italy, for it is clear that there it was brought about by economic reasons rather than the fiscal reasons which may later have become operative. Pliny's letters are illuminating here, in the passages where he deplores the uncultivated fields and the difficulty of finding tenants for them. The emperors made many efforts to protect Italian agriculture, and in particular to encourage a revival of viticulture. But the competition from the provinces proved too much. The entire population of Italy was living off the Empire, and this is what brought about its downfall. Moreover, political unrest, confiscations and uprisings were aggravating an already dangerous situation. That is the reason that the state tended more and more to turn the free peasant into a serf who was tied to the soil, for the interests of the state at this point coincided with those of the large landowners who were short of labour.

5

Large Landowners and Rural Slavery

THE parallel which we have been attempting to establish between Greece and Rome, deriving from the common character of their civilisations which are linked to the life of the city-state, will feature once again in this chapter which is based upon an analysis of two well-known texts, Xenophon's *Oeconomicus* and Cato's *De Agricultura*. These two works describe the same type of farming, on estates of medium size incorporating the cultivation of various kinds of crops, and employing about ten slaves who worked under the supervision of an overseer who was himself a slave. But while this sort of exploitation may have been typical of the larger holdings in both Greece and Rome within the confines of the city-state, it should be remembered that there were also other kinds of large estates and other forms of servile labour in the countryside. During the last years of the Republic Italy had its *latifundia*, with great gangs of slaves. As for Greece, although there were no equally vast estates there, other forms of rural slavery of a rather special kind did exist. These have sometimes been described as serfdom,[1] and the example of the Spartan helots is no doubt better known than most. Our survey must take account of these variations.

1. THE IDEAL ESTATE: ISCHOMACHUS AND CATO

Treatises on agriculture do not appear until quite late on in the history of the ancient cities. It is striking that they almost always concern the cultivation of relatively modest estates which need no more than about ten

---

[1] *Cf.* pages 71–4 on the use of this term.

people to work them. This was clearly the model of a large estate in the context of the ancient city.

The large landowner whom Xenophon describes in the *Oeconomicus* appears to be typical of the fourth-century Athenian society which emerged from the disturbances following the Peloponnesian War. When the war ended Ischomachus' father speculated by buying uncultivated land cheaply, and later, when he had put it back under cultivation, selling it again to *nouveaux riches* who were anxious to acquire the respectability which the possession of landed property still conferred in fourth-century Athens. No doubt he already owned some inherited land, and we may assume that he did not sell off all the newly purchased land, so that Ischamachus' estate was partly composed of these new acquisitions. There is not much detailed information about this estate. Xenophon does not bother to say where it is, nor does he tell us whether it was all in one piece, or, as is probable, composed of parcels of land scattered through several demes in Attica. At all events it was small enough for Ischomachus to be able to visit all of it in a single day, and to inspect, at close hand, the progress of the agricultural work. Even if he had a residence in town, the large landowner in Attica in the fourth century was still a countryman, but a countryman who was not a peasant. While the peasant, even if he had one or two slaves, shared personally in the work in the fields, the large landowner did no more than check on the work of his slaves.

Although the slaves were numerous enough, Xenophon does not provide any figures. Some devoted their time more particularly to domestic tasks. These were, for the most part, women who worked under the direction of the lady of the house. Then there were the agricultural labourers working in the fields, and they sowed, reaped, took in the harvest, pruned the vines and prepared the wine. They appear to have been quite well treated: Ischomachus advises his young wife to take good care of them if they are ill (VII, 37), and tells his overseer to reward them for good work. No doubt, in acting in this way Ischomachus, or rather Xenophon who puts the words into his mouth, is obeying a moral impulse. However, it is also a question of the considered interest of the master of the estate: well treated slaves work better, and this is to everybody's advantage. The slaves are fed, clothed, and housed by their master, and, as a rule, receive no pay. Ischomachus acquires clothes and shoes of varying qualities and gives the best ones to the most efficient workers and the remainder to the others (XIII, 10). However, this individual touch of rewarding the best efforts is prompted by Xenophon's own ideas on ethics, and no doubt masters possessing a large number of slaves had all their clothes and shoes made alike. But it seems likely that this type of pay in kind was occasionally supplemented by some financial remuneration which made it possible for the slave to save a small sum of money and maybe buy his liberty. Attested examples are rare of rural slaves being freed, except by wills, and it is hard to tell what the situation really was. We may also suppose that slaves sometimes indulged in petty larceny in an attempt to improve their everyday life.

Xenophon's *Oeconomicus* also gives details about the way the slaves were lodged. The house would have two rooms for this purpose, one dormitory for the men and one for the women. Ischomachus takes good care to keep them separate to avoid the possibility of slave families, which shows that despite his apparent solicitude for them, he did not consider them to be quite human beings.

Two figures who held an important position stand out from the rest of the slaves on the estate: the housekeeper, who supervised the work of the women in the house, and the overseer who directed the work of the men in the fields. These two were in very close contact with the master and his wife. The housekeeper was responsible for the care of all the articles which were used only for special occasions—the processional robes, precious vases, painted pottery, and so on. She also assisted the mistress in her principal task which was to apportion the work and keep order in the house. The overseer had to deputise for the master whenever the master could not be present. Ischomachus is often called away to town on business or to take part in a meeting of the Assembly or to sit on a jury. Moreover, since his lands were probably not all in the same deme, he would need several overseers who could distribute the work among the slaves and supervise them.

In the *Oeconomicus* the overseers are themselves slaves. But we know from other sources that in the fourth century men who were free but poverty-stricken were able to hire themselves out as overseers on the estates of a few rich landowners. In Xenophon's *Memorabilia* (II, 8, 3), Socrates suggests that one of his questioners who is complaining of poverty should take this course. The overseer's most necessary quality was the ability to lead other men. Of course, he also had to be familiar with agricultural techniques, but these were not difficult to learn. What mattered most was that the different jobs should be sensibly and rationally divided among the agricultural labourers, and that order and discipline should reign. We may well imagine, although the *Oeconomicus* does not say so explicitly, that overseers did not hesitate to resort to punishment and blows to maintain order, so that the slaves had more to fear from these fellow-slaves than from their master who only supervised them from afar.

It was the rational organisation of the work far more than 'the farmers reputed to have made some clever discovery in agriculture' (*Oeconomicus* XX, 5) which enabled the large landowner to obtain a better yield from his land. In the fourth century, at the time when Xenophon was writing the *Oeconomicus*, there were men in Athens who were no longer satisfied with the rents from their land in the traditional manner but who invested in agriculture in order to increase their fortunes. Most commonly it was a matter of speculation linked to the rise in price of foodstuffs which most made itself felt during the second half of the century. But, already in the *Oeconomicus,* we can see signs of this desire to increase profits by organising work on the estates as rationally as possible.

Cato was influenced by a similar motive at the time that he produced his *De Agricultura.* We know that this Roman statesman, who inveighed so passionately against Rome's imperialistic policies and against the decline in the old Republican tradition, was not only the instigator of the last war against Carthage, but also a speculator and an astute businessman. At all events, being attached to the traditions of the city, the estate that he takes as a model is the same type of estate as Ischomachus', and he ignores the vast *latifundia* which were then being developed in the south of Italy and in Sicily, which employed whole armies of slaves.

Cato is much more precise than Xenophon. He calculates that thirteen people are necessary to work an estate of 240 *jugera* (150 acres) planted with olive trees: one overseer to supervise the work, a housekeeper, five agricultural labourers, three carters, one donkey driver, one swineherd and one shepherd. For a vineyard of 100 *jugera,* he suggests, apart from the overseer and the housekeeper, ten labourers, one carter, one man for the donkeys, one man to supervise the grape harvest, one swineherd—altogether eighteen people. This figure does not include the extra hands hired temporarily for the busiest periods, such as the grape-pickers, *vindemiatores,* who are mentioned in inscriptions. Thus the permanent labour force of the estate remains relatively small. Cato, like Xenophon, is concerned about the way to care for the slaves, how to house, feed and clothe them. Here, too, he is more precise than Xenophon and also less sentimental: 'He must see that the servants are well provided for, and that they do not suffer from cold or hunger' (*De Agricultura* V, 2). And he recommends that the overseer should make them work as hard as possible, as theft and crime are encouraged by idleness.

This type of medium-sized estate was widespread,

especially in central Italy and in Campania, where arboriculture had almost completely taken the place of grain
cultivation. Cato defines the ideal estate as being about
100 *jugera*, and recommends that one should plant first
vines, then vegetables, fruit trees and olive trees, and
lastly, cereals. Just like Xenophon in his *Oeconomicus*,
then, he is describing a profitable type of agriculture
where the best yields are obtained when the tasks of
cultivation are fairly distributed among the staff. A large
proportion of the yield was marketable in the form of oil
or wine. On such estates, excavations have uncovered
near the master's villa special storage places where the
oil and wine, which were later to be sold in the neighbouring town, were kept in large jars called *dolia*. This
type of farming continued in Italy up to the beginning
of the second century A.D. Varro and Columella repeat
Cato's recommendations, altering them hardly at all, and
the estate owned by the poet Horace (*Epistles* I, 16, 1–10)
in the Sabine countryside can be taken to be typical of
this kind of medium-sized property. The portion
reserved for the owner was planted with vines, fruit trees
and wheat, and cultivated by eight slaves working under
the supervision of an overseer. The rest of the estate was
let to five *coloni*, each of whom personally cultivated his
particular allotment of land.

This type of exploitation was to take over everywhere
eventually, during the late Empire. More and more of
the land was let to tenant farmers, while the arboriculture which was becoming ever less profitable was
replaced by grain cultivation once again. For a time,
however, the more scientifically organised agriculture
had achieved its best balance and produced the greatest
yields.

2. LATIFUNDIA

The economy of the *latifundia* was quite different. It
began to be developed in the second century B.C. in the

south of Italy, Sicily, Sardinia, and later in North Africa. It was, in part, the result of the conquests and the immense influx of wealth and manpower which submerged Italy and later the entire West. We know it chiefly through literary descriptions. Its development usually involved some changing over from arboriculture to pastoral farming, and in certain regions such as Sicily or North Africa it led to large-scale grain production aimed at supplying the Italian markets. These were immense estates of many hundreds of acres and were owned by members of the Roman aristocracy, the great senatorial families. A number of these estates were later confiscated and passed into the hands of the emperor after the civil wars, to form the core of the great imperial domains of the second century A.D. At the same time the large private holdings, upon which the power of the Roman aristocracy depended right up till the end of the Empire, did not disappear—witness the estates of Symmachus or of Saint Melania at the beginning of the fifth century.

Needless to say, the owner of such domains as these, which often included land in various provinces, did not reside on his estates. All he did was pocket the income which his bailiffs turned over to him. These bailiffs were very much more important people than the overseers of Cato's *De Agricultura*. Likewise, the slaves who worked on these estates were not counted in tens, but in hundreds or thousands. Most of them came from the East, prisoners of war or human cattle bought in the Aegean markets, especially at Delos, where, according to Strabo (XIV, 5, 2), as many as 10,000 slaves could be turned over in a day. They were nostalgic for their native lands and they could occasionally recall some vague memory of the Hellenistic monarchies whose splendours had left them with a lasting impression. There was no longer any question of considering them as human beings, of treating them with a compassionate but strict justice, nor was there any question of encouraging them to hope for freedom in return for loyal service. They were many and therefore to be feared. They had to be treated as a vanquished foe if they were to be forced into obedience. At the same time, the fact that it was very easy to procure them and that their cost was extremely low, had the effect of positively depriving them of any personal value. They were cattle and were treated as such. Each estate was bound to have its *ergastulum*, the prison where the offenders were locked up. Chains and branding irons were commonplace, as were the most deplorable corporal punishments—torture and crucifixion. The harshness with which they were treated accounts for the great slave revolts which broke out in Sicily and in the south of Italy late in the second century B.C.

Sicily was one of the regions most involved in the development of the *latifundia*. The small estate had, it is true, not entirely disappeared. However, it was not unusual to find there estates of 1,200 acres, such as those mentioned by Cicero in the *Verrines*, which belonged to men like Diocles of Panormus (Palermo) or Nympho of Centuripe, or to Roman citizens like Lucius Bruttius or Caius Martinius. Whole armies of slaves worked on these vast estates. It was on one of them, belonging to a Greek from Enna, named Damophilus, that the first great slave revolt broke out. Its leader was a certain Eunus, from Apamea in Syria, who, once he had made himself master of Enna, styled himself king with the name of Antiochus. The revolt soon affected the entire island, and even some of the Greek cities, Enna, Tauromenium and Morgantina, fell to the insurgents. Three successive expeditions, in 134, 133, and 132, had to be sent before they were crushed.

Rebellion flared up again at the end of the century. Diodorus, who is our main source, relates how it started among the slaves belonging to a Roman knight, Publius Clonius, who had property in the western part of the island. The insurgents soon numbered 6,000 and elected as king Salvius who took the name of Tryphon. Another 'king', Athenion, also appeared in the west; and he was soon at the head of an army of 10,000 slaves and joined forces with Tryphon. This time the revolt was far better organised. Tryphon established his capital at Triocala, in the south-west, and made it into a fortified stronghold. For more than three years, from 104 to 101, the slaves were masters of almost the entire island, with only the towns escaping them. Lucullus tried in vain to overthrow them, and only in 100 did the consul Aquilius manage to seize Triocala, an unidentified town in the south-west, and the last of its defenders.

Unlike the first two slave wars, the third and most famous of them, led by Spartacus, did not break out in Sicily but in Campania, and it did not start among the rural slaves but among the gladiators. However it very quickly spread to the rural areas of southern Italy, and soon Spartacus had an army of 70,000 men. On this occasion, too, Rome had to mount a large military operation before it could crush the revolt, and Crassus was for a long time held off by the slaves. Spartacus' revolt lasted from 73 to 71, and his defeat marked the end of the great slave wars. Other places besides Italy had been affected. Similar outbreaks had occurred in Greece and in Asia, but unfortunately we know very little about them. With the exception of the revolt in the Laurium mines in Attica, at the end of the second century, it is noteworthy that these uprisings occurred mostly among the rural slaves working on the large estates which were so much a feature of the Roman conquered territory.

From the later years of the Republic onwards there was a decline in farming of the *latifundia* type. The concentration of the ownership of estates, which continued during the early centuries of the Empire, no longer necessarily entailed the development of large-scale farms and a massive use of slave labour. The great slave revolts had shown that it was dangerous to concentrate too many slaves in one place. It would appear that the Romans henceforth allowed local types of farming to continue when they acquired new territory: in Egypt, Asia Minor and Syria the village communities of small free tenants remained, paying a rent to the Roman who owned the land, the emperor himself or a private individual. Even in Gaul and Spain free peasants remained one of the fundamental elements of the rural population. They were, of course, burdened with heavy taxes and military obligations over and above the payment of land rent, and in fact their lot was close to that of servitude from an economic point of view. However, under the law they remained free men, at least until the late Empire.

Thus, what took place from the first years of the Empire onwards was an eclipse of the rural economy based upon the *latifundia* and dependent upon a vast slave labour force. It is true that until the last days of the Empire there were still some large domains worked by gangs of slaves under the supervision of bailiffs. But from the second century A.D. onwards in Italy, and from the third century in the rest of the Empire, it became more and more the custom, even on medium-sized estates, to keep only a small number of slaves on the 'reserved' farm, and to hand over the remainder, in small allotments, to free tenants, or even to slaves. The final result was a general system based upon the colonate. Paradoxically, the late Empire thus returned to the type of farming which had predominated in certain parts of the Greek world well before the Roman conquest, and which, although it was fundamentally different, has a certain apparent resemblance to medieval serfdom.

3. 'SERFDOM' IN ANTIQUITY: THE SPARTAN HELOTS AND OTHER FORMS OF SERVILE DEPENDENCE

The term 'serfdom' is frequently used by modern writers to describe a type of servile dependence which was substantially different from classical slavery, and which existed in certain parts of the Greek world. The ancient writers described both these forms of servitude by the same Greek word, *douleia,* which defined the legal status of the slave. At a much later date some writers, such as the lexicographer Pollux, spoke of an intermediary status between that of the slave and that of the free man. In fact, this type of servile dependence was only to be found in some places among the Greeks, and seemed to reflect a special situation which arose from military conquest. In Laconia and Messenia, the Dorian conquest had reduced the original Greek population to the condition of helots. The Klarotae in Crete, the Bithynii of Byzantium, the Mariandyni of Heraclea Pontica, and the Penestae in Thessaly were similarly the descendants of the original occupants of the land, reduced into servitude by conquerors with superior military power, and forced then to cultivate for them land which had previously been their own. Given that these slaves of a special kind were peasants, and that they were compelled to pay heavy dues to their masters, can we call them serfs? They were, in fact, as different from the medieval serf as from the slave belonging to one of Aristophanes' peasants.

We are less ill-informed about the Spartan helots and the Klarotae of Crete than about the others. The Spartan constitution laid down that each citizen should receive at birth an allotment of land to provide for his needs. All these *kleroi* were worked by the helots, during the Classical period at least. These helots were obliged to pay a fixed due in kind to the master of the *kleros*. They were then free to dispose of the surplus as they wished. Moreover, the helots did not belong to individual Spartans, but to the community as a whole which alone had the power to free them. For these reasons, they themselves formed a close-knit community, and this explains how it was that so many revolts broke out among the helots, often endangering the security of Sparta. The Cretan Klarotae, on the other hand, belonged to individual masters, but we know from the law-code of Gortyn that the Klarotae, there called *oikēes*, were allowed to possess a house, cattle and tools, to have a family, and to pass on their possessions when they died. Legally, of course, neither the helots nor the Klarotae were free men. The most harsh corporal punishments

72

were inflicted upon them if they were found to be at fault. The Spartan helot was universally despised and was forced to submit to the most appalling mistreatment, for instance through the *krypteia* which so aroused the indignation of Athenian writers. (The *krypteia* was an institution about which we know very little, but it involved, in particular, a man-hunt in which the helots were the victims.) Finally, neither the helots nor the Klarotae had any political rights; they were not members of the city-community. For this reason they did not serve in the army except as batmen, and only in the most exceptional circumstances was their help called upon. It is worth noting, however, that in the case of the helots this did occasionally happen, particularly during the Peloponnesian War (Thucydides, IV, 80).

In the context of our particular subject, labour, these slaves were first and foremost peasants, but despite what has often been asserted, this form of servile dependence was not necessarily linked to the large-estate system. In Sparta, Crete and even around Syracuse, the helots, Klarotae, and Kyllyrioi appear to have been individual tenants, cultivating a small plot of land, although this plot may have been part of a larger estate. Attempts have been made to calculate the size of the Spartan *kleros*, on the basis of the few figures which have been handed down to us by ancient authors: estimates vary between seventeen and ninety acres. Even if we work on the latter figure, which is no doubt exaggerated, we may still take it that each helot received a portion of this *kleros* with the responsibility of cultivating it. Perhaps they may be called large estates, but except in Thessaly where horses were reared on vast domains, these large estates were seldom exploited as single units. So forms of dependence similar to the Spartan helot-system were also to be found in areas where small holdings predominated.

These forms of dependence, about which, unfortunately, we know very little, appear to have changed fairly rapidly. In Sparta, from the fourth century B.C. onwards, there were ordinary slaves as well as the helots.

In Thessaly, the Penestae obtained their freedom at the end of the fifth or the beginning of the fourth century. In Syracuse, there were no more Kyllyrioi after the tyranny of Dionysius I (405–367 B.C.), who granted them citizenship. We do not know what became of the Bithynii or the Mariandyni, but during the period of the Roman Empire communities of free peasants existed in these areas, so we may suppose that, as the memory of their initial defeat faded, these communities of peasants shook off their ancient servitude. They seldom obtained full ownership of the land they cultivated. More often they remained obliged to pay heavy dues to the owners of the soil, whether these were *curiales* of the neighbouring city or Roman conquerors. Still, these communities were typical of a kind of rural economy which lived on after the Roman conquest.

The ancient world, the world of the city-state, thus incorporated quite a number of different forms of rural labour. While the citizen farmer who owned his land remained the ideal, this did not exclude the existence of many other types of agricultural workers who were legally dependent on others to a greater or lesser extent. And between Ischomachus and the owner of the great *latifundia* of the late Empire there was an infinite variety of large landowners. Agricultural labour was the chief activity of the greater part of the population all around the Mediterranean. Agriculture soon changed from being only a way of earning a livelihood to being also a way of producing marketable goods. However, the commercialisation of agricultural produce hardly ever altered the agrarian structure in any significant way, and in the final analysis, the ancient peasant, whether free man or slave, changed very little over the centuries.

Part Three

ARTISANS

In the ancient city-state the artisan did not hold a position comparable to that of the peasant, and yet, paradoxically, we know more about the artisan class. The first reason is that certain articles produced by the craftsmen of antiquity have survived to our day. Secondly, since life in the city-state was essentially an urban one focused around the Agora and the Forum, ancient literature tells us more about the life of the urban plebs. Moreover, excavations have uncovered actual workshops about which we can form a fairly clear idea. Finally, by very reason of their low social status, the artisans were quick to form associations of a religious and professional nature, and these left behind a wealth of evidence, both written and pictorial, about their activities.

This last remark, it should be said, applies especially to the Roman world. Until the Hellenistic age there was nothing comparable in the Greek world. Nor do we possess much information about the Roman artisan class until quite a late period, from the second century A.D. onwards. It is therefore impossible to undertake a general description which can apply both to the world of the Greek city-states and to Rome. We shall return to the reasons for this difference, but it seems at the outset possible to connect them with the change that took place in the third century B.C. First, the conquests of Alexander and then the conquests of Rome destroyed the ideal of self-sufficiency in the Greek world, which was linked to the limited demand for the products of the artisan.

6

Artisans in the Greek Cities

THE artisans as a clearly defined social group make a relatively late appearance in the Greek world. For a long time their crafts were a part of domestic life. It is true that the *demiourgoi* were a feature of Mycenaean society, but they worked in the context of a palace economy about which we know very little. At the time when the Greek world was at last emerging from the centuries of obscurity which had followed the destruction of the Mycenaean civilisation there still seem to have been very few artisans. The Homeric poems mention the carpenter, the blacksmith, the potter, the man who builds houses and ships, the man who makes arms, and the man who produces vases for daily use and also the big funeral urns which were luxury articles. This production had a purely local market, being designed simply to satisfy the needs of the city's inhabitants, and particularly those of the warriors who were at this time the ruling class.

Gradually, demand became diversified. Although the colonisation movement during the eighth and seventh centuries was not, as is now generally agreed, undertaken with a commercial purpose, it nevertheless served to establish a vast network of exchanges. Although these exchanges usually took the form of simple barter, the system allowed the mother-cities to acquire the raw materials which they needed, chiefly foodstuffs and also metal; and at the same time it opened up a much wider market for the products made in Corinth, Rhodes and later Athens. The first appearance of coinage, towards the end of the seventh century, speeded up these exchanges; although the coins were themselves still commodities as well as means of exchange, when they were monopolised by certain cities they helped establish almost absolute control over the countries producing raw materials and especially foodstuffs. In some cities this ability to import foodstuffs, above all wheat, on a large scale precipitated an agrarian crisis, which had many complex causes and which was solved in various ways. One consequence was to provide the emerging body of artisans, whose wares were increasingly in demand, with a labour force made available by the lack of land.

Once again, it is only for Athens that there is enough evidence to take us beyond mainly hypothetical arguments. In that city, it is almost certain that the artisans began to play a role in the life of the city from the beginning of the sixth century B.C. It has been suggested that this was one of the consequences of the half-measures brought into operation by Solon, which contributed towards the creation of a 'proletariat' of men who were free but uprooted. Whether or not this is a correct explanation, there is no disputing that the role of the urban *demos* became increasingly important during the decades following Solon, and that among the numerous *thetes* there were manual labourers engaged in a *techne*, a skilled trade. On the other hand, it has been shown that there were not more than 400 ceramic workers in Athens in the fifth century, the period when red-figured ware reached its highest point of achievement. The historian should, then, be cautious in his conclusions and beware of overestimating the importance of the artisan class in the ancient cities.

Nevertheless, it is possible to form a picture of the Athenian artisan class at the end of the fifth century B.C. and in the fourth, when literary sources, inscriptions, and the archaeological remains become more numerous. Economic, social and political developments had by then introduced more diversification into the social structure. The Empire had opened up new markets for Athens; the coinage of Athens was predominant in the Aegean world which its triremes controlled; the Acropolis was covered with monuments to the glory of the gods who protected the state, above all, Athena. Among the leisured classes, dress and jewellery were becoming more sophisticated, especially for women, and rich Athenians coming together at a banquet liked to see beautiful table services. There was still, it is true, an important home industry: in Ischomachus' house the servants span and wove the cloth from which were made the clothes for the entire household. But although the domestic crafts were still quite important, contemporary sources give ample evidence that manufacture had become an autonomous activity needing more and more workers. There is a well-known passage in Plato's *Republic* (369 B *ff*), in which Socrates explains the advantages to be gained from a division of labour within the city, and an equally famous one in Xenophon's *Cyropaedia* (VIII, 2, 5):

> In small towns the same workman makes chairs and doors and ploughs and tables, and often this same artisan builds houses, and even so he is thankful if he can only find employment enough to support him. And it is, of course, impossible for a man of many trades to be proficient in all of them. In large cities, on the other hand, inasmuch as many people have demands to make upon each branch of industry, one trade alone, and very often even less than a whole trade, is enough to support a man: one man, for instance, makes shoes for men, and another for women; and there are places even where one man earns a living by only stitching shoes, another by cutting them out, another by sewing the uppers together, while there is another who performs none of these operations but only assembles the parts.

Perhaps there were in Athens cobblers' workshops which suggested this comparison to Xenophon. At all events it is significant that he should have been capable of realising so clearly the link between the development of the artisan class and the law of supply and demand.

What then were the main industries in Athens during

the Classical period?[1] Mining, the first industry to be considered, stands apart from the others. Even more than pottery, it provided the Athenian traders with their chief export—the coins which were still in great demand during the fourth century and which never varied in quality. The deposits of silver lead at Laurium began to be worked in the sixth century, but it was only from the first decades of the fifth century that the industry reached its peak with the discovery of the rich veins of Maronea. From information provided by the excavations at Laurium at the end of the nineteenth century, and from Diodorus' famous descriptions of work in the Spanish and Egyptian mines in the Roman period (V, 38; III, 13), we can reconstruct a picture of the mining industry. It involved two separate operations, first extracting the ore, and secondly treating it in workshops on the surface. The ore was smelted on the spot; remains of furnaces have actually been found near mining seams. Most of the mining was open-cast. However, there were also some underground seams, and their maintenance appears to have left much to be desired: a legal speech from the fourth century (Plutarch, *Lives of the Ten Orators, Lycurgus*, 34) mentions pillars of ore which had been left as supports, and the accusation is made that one greedy concession-holder, a certain Diphilus, had not hesitated to work them, at the risk of causing the collapse of the mine. The interpretation put upon Diphilus' action has, however, been questioned. We know from other sources that wood was imported for use as props in the mines, and it has therefore been suggested that the pillars of ore which Diphilus destroyed served rather to mark the boundaries between the various concessions. Whatever the explanation may be, conditions of work

[1] For the most part our sources come from the end of the fifth century but even more from the fourth century. This means that some elements in the description which follows are especially applicable to the crisis period following the Peloponnesian War. Other aspects are, however, common to both the fifth and the fourth centuries as a whole.

must have been wretched. The miner worked most of the time lying flat, in semi-darkness, and although traces have been found of a system of ventilation to prevent the men dying of suffocation, the fate of those who worked in the mines could hardly have been an enviable one.

The mines belonged to the Athenian state, who let out concessions to individuals on payment of a fee. At least this appears to have been the general rule from the evidence of many inscriptions, nearly all of which date from the third quarter of the fourth century B.C. when there was a brief revival in the mining industry. Arguments have been put forward to support the theory that some mines were sold outright by the state, so that private mines existed alongside those divided up into state concessions. However, this view remains questionable.

The rental paid by the concession-holder was a very modest one. Of seventy-six fees recorded on surviving inscriptions, twenty-two are for twenty drachmas, thirty for 150 drachmas, and even the highest does not exceed 6,000 drachmas. In the legal speeches the figures mentioned are somewhat higher; Demosthenes in *Against Pantaenetus* (XXXVII, 31) refers to a concession comprising three separate parts, the total value of which reached three talents (18,000 drachmas). However, these are isolated examples, and we should not be misled by them: in the fourth century at least, the concessions must generally have been relatively small, probably restricted to one gallery. They were not all of the same kind, nor did they last for the same length of time. In the *Constitution of Athens* (XLVII, 2), Aristotle makes a distinction between two types of concession, the *ergasima* and the *synkechoremena*. The former were mines already being worked: they were let out for a period of three years. The *synkechoremena*, sometimes called *anasaxima* or *palaia anasaxima* in inscriptions, were mines which were not yet being operated, or which had ceased to be in operation for some time; concessions were valid for seven years. Aristotle does not say, and we do not know,

81

whether the rental-fee was paid annually or once only at the time when the concession was assigned.

Despite the relatively small fees, it is remarkable that the concession-holders named in inscriptions and legal speeches are rich men who, in many cases, possessed workshops and real estate in the mining areas as well as their mining concession. Some were politicians known from other evidence to have performed liturgies, including the most important of them, the trierarchy. Another striking fact revealed by the inscriptions is that it was not rare for the son of a concession-holder to take one himself a few years later. And virtually all of them were citizens. It is striking that the metics, foreigners living in Athens who were active in the industry and commerce of the city, do not appear among the surviving lists of concession-holders. The sole exception may be Sosias, a Thracian to whom, according to Xenophon (*Ways and Means* IV, 14), the wealthy Nicias rented out a thousand slaves in the fifth century. But according to another plausible interpretation Sosias was merely the overseer to whom Nicias paid the considerable sum of one talent to organise and operate his mines, while he himself devoted his time to politics and war (Xenophon, *Memorabilia* II, 5, 2).

Xenophon provides us with valuable information about work in the mines in his *Ways and Means*, which he wrote towards the middle of the fourth century, at a time when the exploitation of the Laurium mines was undergoing a definite decline. The labour force was almost entirely composed of slaves, although occasionally a free man might also have shouldered a pick; at least this is what one legal speech of the fourth century leads one to believe. How many slaves worked at Laurium altogether? It is a difficult question to answer as there are no recorded figures. Besides, the mining industry was not equally vigorous at all times; there was in particular a definite drop in production during the Peloponnesian War and in the early decades of the fourth century. This slow-down can be explained in part by the war itself. Thucydides (VII, 27, 5) records that 20,000 slaves, many of them working in the mines, had fled after the occupation of Decelea by the Spartans in 413. Does this figure represent the entire slave labour force working in the mines or only a proportion, and if so, how great a proportion? It is not possible to give any firm answer to these questions. In the fourth century, when Xenophon in the *Ways and Means* is considering upon what conditions activity in the mines might be renewed, he goes so far as to suggest that the state should buy three slave-miners to every one Athenian citizen. If one estimates that there were at this time about 30,000 Athenian citizens, it is clear that Xenophon was contemplating using an extremely large number of slaves in the mines and in the surface workshops connected with them. However, it is unlikely that such a figure was ever reached; not only was there never the slightest move to put Xenophon's plan into operation, but there was never at any one time such a large concentration of men at Laurium.

Sometimes the concession-holder would use his own slaves, either under his personal supervision if only a small team was involved, or under the direction of one or several overseers if the force was larger. But the most common practice was to hire slaves. According to Xenophon (*Ways and Means* IV, 14–16):

Nicias, son of Niceratus, once owned 1,000 men in the mines and let them out to Sosias the Thracian, on condition that Sosias paid him an obol[1] a day per man net and filled all vacancies as they occurred. Hipponicus, again, had 600 slaves let out on the same terms and received a rent of a mina[1] a day net. Philemonides had 300, and received half a mina. There were others too, owning numbers in proportion, I presume, to their capital. But why dwell on the past? At this day there are many men in the mines let out in this way.

[1] See Appendix II—Ancient Monetary Equivalents.

One of Andocides' speeches (*Mysteries*, 38) indicates that it was not necessary to be as rich as Nicias, Philemonides, or Hipponicus to be able to go in for hiring out slave-miners: a certain Dioclides had just one slave working for someone else in Laurium who brought him in his daily obol. The advantages of this system are obvious: the concession-holder who was just starting to mine a seam was able to acquire a large labour force without paying too large a sum at the outset for the purchase of slaves; the slave-owner was assured of an income and the purchase of slaves thus took the form of a good investment which Xenophon suggested to the Athenian state as a means to increase its revenues. His suggestion has been the subject of much discussion. It would be ridiculous to see it as a plan for the rational and systematic exploitation of the mines by the state. Xenophon was simply working from the observation of two factors. Money is a commodity of which one cannot have too much—'No one ever yet possessed so much silver as to want no more; if a man finds himself with a huge amount of it, he takes as much pleasure in burying the surplus as in using it.' (*Ways and Means* IV, 7)—and the uses of money are obvious. The silver mines should therefore be exploited to the maximum. Secondly, there are men in Athens who grow rich by hiring out slaves. Why then should the Athenian state too not buy slaves and hire them out to the concession-holders, thus ensuring a regular income for itself? Furthermore, the state could in this way act as an entrepreneur without eliminating private enterprise, and the Athenians would thus share in the profits of a collective exploitation of the mines, without running the risk of making a bad investment. Was the project in fact practicable? Xenophon certainly believed that it was, for he examined, with a wealth of unexpected detail, the practical methods of buying slaves and the different stages of the entire operation. But whatever his supposed or effective influence on the men who ran the city may have been, Xenophon never saw his project carried out.

Nevertheless, the mines continued to be worked throughout the fourth century, and even after the defeat of Chaeronea skilful prospectors could still make substantial fortunes from mining. As for the miners themselves, the slaves who could be hired out at considerable profit, they lived a wretched life near the mines, but were not committed to the service of one single master, and this afforded them a relative measure of independence in their work and even in their lives. The position was probably similar for the slaves who worked in the surface workshops, the *ergasteria*, which were very often owned by the same men who held concessions in the pits. Sometimes, though, the workshops belonged to other citizens who no doubt bought from the concession-holders the crude ore which they then transformed. These workshops varied greatly in size. On their sites have been found furnaces and mortars, as well as the tubs in which the ore was washed. Polybius (XXXIV, 9) gives a description of the operations by which the silver ore was reduced in the Spanish mines, and it is certainly valid for Laurium too:

... the lumps of silver ore which are washed down by the streams are crushed, and passed through sieves into water. The deposit is then again crushed and sifted and while the water is running off undergoes a third crushing. This is done five times in all and the fifth deposit, after the lead has been drained off, produces pure silver.

This, then, appears to have been how the mining industry in Athens was organised in the fourth century, the century about which we know most. There were other mines in the Greek world, but for these we have only the most fragmentary and disjointed information. It is likely that, as at Laurium, the labour force was chiefly composed of slaves who lived and worked in equally wretched conditions which remained largely unchanged throughout antiquity.

A second industry about which we possess valuable

information is public works, including the shipyards.[1] Here again, a tight control was exercised by the city. When a project had been approved in principle by the people voting in the Assembly, a commission of *epistatai* was appointed, who, working in close contact with the Council, drew up the specifications and concluded a series of individual contracts with the various suppliers of materials, with the contractors and with the workmen themselves. An architect was generally responsible for co-ordinating the different operations, as did Callicrates and Ictinus in the case of the Parthenon, Koroibos and Metagenes at Eleusis, and Callicrates again for the Long Walls linking Athens and the Piraeus (Plutarch, *Pericles*, 13). There were possibly two categories of architects, especially from the fourth century onwards: the private architects who worked according to contracts drawn up with the city, after the city had approved their plan or *syngraphe*; and the state architects, civil servants in a sense, who apparently received a lower salary. The latter included in particular those who were responsible for the maintenance of public buildings. Their salary seems to have been ridiculously low, a drachma and a half to two drachmas a day, sometimes even less, which means that they received barely more than a skilled workman, a stone-cutter, for instance.

The architects then were, with the exception of a few outstanding personalities, simply technicians. They were often responsible for recruiting workers, and at a later period, at least, it was not unusual for the architect to accompany his team of skilled workmen wherever they went. These skilled workers—stone-cutters, sculptors, carpenters and smiths—received a wage which was fixed in advance in the contract. It might be in the form of a daily wage or else a flat sum paid for a specific task, for instance the fluting of columns. It was sometimes a payment in kind—food and clothes equivalent to three obols per day—and in some cases, but not invariably, a mone-

[1] See Appendix I.

tary payment was added. In Athens this varied from one drachma at the end of the fifth century to a drachma and a half at the end of the fourth century, paid on completion of the particular job.

What was the legal status of these building workers? Again the inscriptions provide us with fascinating details. Taking only Athens into consideration, in 409 B.C., of 71 workers under contract on the Erechtheum, 20 were Athenian citizens, and the rest slaves or metics. Six teams of men who redressed the stonework of the columns are mentioned; of them, 7 were citizens (of whom 3 were foremen), 6 were metics (2 foremen) and 21 were slaves (one of whom, Onesimus, was a foreman). In the Eleusis records of 329, there were 21 citizens among the 94 skilled workers, 9 among the 27 contractors, 11 among the 41 suppliers. Whether they were citizens, metics or slaves, all the workers received the same pay. And although there were more slaves than free men, there was nothing comparable to the enormous gangs of slaves who built the Egyptian pyramids.

It is reasonable to suppose that the pay received by the slaves on the one hand and the free men on the other was only equal in appearance. The slave never retained his whole wage for himself, whether he worked alongside his master, who might himself be a tradesman, or whether he belonged to a master who either hired him out directly to a contractor or left him free to hire himself out. Assuredly, as in the case of the *choris oikountes* to be considered later, he had to hand over some of his pay to his master. When the total wage for a team was paid to its foreman, he withheld from the pay of the slave a sum of money to cover his hire and his upkeep, unless the city itself provided the latter. Among the building workers there were also slaves who belonged to the state, and these were simply allowed a sum of three obols per day to cover their food (*trophe*). All in all, as in the mines, there does not appear to have been any generally standard procedure for hiring labour, and private enterprise took an active part in public works through-out the Classical period.

Despite the important part played by public buildings in the life of a Greek city, the building industry does not seem to have differed substantially from any other occupation of the artisan class, except for the fact that the state exercised control over it. The same is true for shipbuilding, which held an important place in Athens' industrial activity. Here again, most of our knowledge concerns the administrative side of the industry. We know from Aristotle (*Constitution of Athens*, XLVI, 1) how the city would come to a decision to undertake the con-struction of ships. The Council chose ten *trieropoioi* who were responsible for recruiting designers (also called 'architects') and for putting contracts for building the ships to public tender. The successful contractors were known as *naupegoi*. It is significant that in many cases, as recorded on surviving inscriptions, they were also trierarchs, that is, they were recruited from amongst the rich Athenians or metics to whom the state entrusted the manning and command of a trireme. The labour force must have been composed of both free workers and slaves, as in the case of the building trade. The workers received their materials from the contractors and were probably paid at piece rates. One or more designers supervised the work. The yards themselves were state-owned, and the state entrusted them to the care of special officers called *epimeletai*.

One conclusion emerges from this analysis of the three industries which developed greatly during the Classical period in Athens, and in other Greek cities which were religious centres, such as Delos or Delphi, or centres of commerce like Corinth: the only concentra-tion of industry that occurred in the Greek cities was geographical, as in the mines of Laurium, or merely temporary, as in the case of various ambitious public-works programmes. Work carried on by the individual craftsman retained the usual pattern.

This observation is even more true of the other

industries. One of the most important of these was metallurgy, a very ancient craft which had split off from domestic industry at an early date. Its importance was accounted for by the necessities of war—the improvement of weapons and the equipment of mercenary armies. Particularly striking is the fact that the largest known concentration in single workshops occurred in the armaments industry. The workshop belonging to Cephalus, the father of Lysias the orator, employed 120 slaves; the one belonging to Demosthenes' father employed thirty slaves in the manufacture of arms and knives, and the workshop making shields which belonged to the rich banker Pasion was of a comparable size. Although some exaggeration may be allowed for in Aristophanes' comedies, it is certainly not without reason that he depicts the complaints of the arms manufacturers when the peasants are successful in their call for peace (in the play of the same name) under the leadership of Trygaeus, a vine-cultivator. Similarly the distinctions Aristophanes draws among the armourers, between the makers of helmets, crests, swords, and pikes, are not purely comic exaggerations. The armaments industry was, in Athens certainly, one of those to which the famous passage on the division of labour in Xenophon's *Cyropaedia* was most relevant. The examples already mentioned indicate that the workshops were indeed very specialised: Cephalus and Pasion made only shields, Demosthenes' father only weapons with cutting edges. A certain Pistias mentioned in Xenophon's *Memorabilia* (III, 10, 9) was reputed for the quality of his breastplates, a fact which allowed him to charge all the more for them. Another characteristic of the armaments industry was that arms were not simply made to order, but there were stockpiles of both raw materials and finished products, which was understandable, since there was an assured and constant market for these products. When the so-called Thirty Tyrants seized Cephalus' workshop, they found 700 shields stored there. Similarly, when Demosthenes' father died, he left in his workshop raw materials such as ivory, iron, and bronze, which the greedy guardians of his children promptly laid hands upon.

As regards the organisation of the actual work, most of our information comes from the three legal speeches made against his guardians by Demosthenes. The workshop usually adjoined the master's house. The workers, all slaves, worked under the direction of an overseer who was himself a slave, and who apportioned the work and supervised the feeding and lodging of the slaves. Unlike some who were employed on public building sites, these slaves received no payment, only a *trophe*. They belonged to the master armourer, who could sell them or employ them as he wished. They probably lived in the master's house.

That is not to say that there were no free men in the metal trades. Pistias, the breastplate manufacturer who talked to Socrates about the quality of his work, did not simply supervise the work of his slaves from a distance as did Cephalus or Demosthenes' father, but took part himself in the manufacture of the articles produced in his workshop. Others had only a small workshop where they worked on their own or together with a single slave. Some slaves, known as *choris oikountes*, that is, living outside their master's house, could even practise the profession of smith or toolmaker in a shop entrusted to them by their master. This was the case of the bald smith in Plato's *Republic* (495 E), who became rich enough to buy his liberty and aspire to the hand of his master's daughter. As for the men who owned the workshops, they could equally well be metics, as was Cephalus, or citizens, as were Demosthenes' father and also Pasion after his naturalisation. Among them there were some of those rich citizens who were distrusted by the philosophers and who were influential in determining the imperialistic policies of the city.

The case of the tanners is comparable. We know of at least three famous tanners in classical Athens: Cleon, the demagogue who succeeded Pericles; Anytus, the prosecutor of Socrates and one of the restorers of Athenian democracy at the beginning of the fourth century; and Timarchus, the friend of Demosthenes. All three were politicians who derived from leather workshops operated by slaves the income which allowed them to participate in and even direct city affairs. It is doubtful whether they themselves managed their workshops, even if Aristophanes does make great play of the nauseating tannery smell emanating from the demagogue who was his contemporary and one of the main butts of his mockery. The tanneries belonging to Cleon and to Anytus worked on raw leather, whereas Timarchus' slaves were cobblers under a foreman who was himself a slave. Aeschines (*Against Timarchus*, 97) says that Timarchus earned two obols per day for each slave and three for the foreman. Does this mean that Timarchus was content to make a profit by hiring out his slaves, having rented the workshop lock, stock and barrel to a cobbler artisan? It was a surprisingly large workshop, with nine or ten slaves, which must have made cheap sandals, maybe for slaves and soldiers.

More often the cobblers were small artisans working in their little shops near the Agora, to the orders of their clients. There is a picture of just such a cobbler in a vase-painting (*Plate* II). One wishes that there were more such pictures, but scenes from mythology or of the games provided more elevated subjects for the clients of the pottery industry, which should be ranked with metallurgy and leather work as one of the most important crafts in classical Athens. It was from the middle of the sixth century that Attic pottery, first with black and later with red figures, rapidly became, together with the coins of Athens, one of the principal exchange commodities available to Athenian merchants. Even in the fourth century, when there was clearly a fall in the quantity as well as the quality of Attic vases produced, exports of Athenian pottery still dominated certain regions in the Mediterranean world, especially around the Black Sea.

91

The output was very large, although it is impossible to make any accurate estimates, and certain types of vases showed a marked stability. For these two reasons, some people have described the Athenian ceramic industry in terms of an industrial concentration. But it was really more of a geographical concentration, in the quarter of the city known as the Kerameikos, north-west of the Agora, where all the workshops and kilns of the potters were to be found. The few vase-paintings showing potters at work give us some idea of the working conditions (*see Plate* III). Some of these workshops were quite large, and the master would work there with his slaves. The master himself would usually work at the wheel while his slaves modelled the clay, prepared the lacquers and the glaze, put the vases in the kiln and supervised the firing. Some kilns were probably shared by several workshops. The painter, who was sometimes also the potter but sometimes a different craftsman, as can be seen from the signatures on the vases, was, like the potter, usually a free man. These signatures and some of the remarks made by the comic poets indicate that, in the Classical period, there were still many foreigners among the potters. However, we also know the names of certain citizens who were in the ceramic trade, such as the demagogue Hyperbolus, who was a lamp-maker, or the brother of the orator Aeschines, who was a painter of vases. In Hyperbolus' case it is probable that, like Cleon, he simply supervised his lamp workshop from a distance and left the task of directing his workers to a slave foreman. Anyway, Hyperbolus manufactured lamps, that is, ordinary mass-produced articles. The potter who himself worked at his wheel and signed his pots was, on the other hand, like our modern potters, an artist as much as an artisan. The general pattern was thus very similar to that of the armament industry or of the leather industry: a quite small workshop which served also as a shop; a labour force composed of slaves who worked alongside the master in the smaller workshops, or under the direction of a slave overseer in the large ones.

These remarks could equally well apply to the many other trades which abounded in a city like Athens, and which are mentioned in Aristophanes' plays. These were small enterprises run by poor citizens, by metics or by *choris oikountes*, slaves like the perfumer who had his little shop in the Agora and who is the subject of a legal speech made by Hypereides. It is hard to differentiate between them and the trades already mentioned. The difference is one of scale rather than structure. The small craftsman working at home, alone or with the help of a slave, carrying his wares to market or selling them in his little shop near the Agora, was a familiar figure in the Greek city. In Athens it was these small craftsmen who made up the majority of those present at the meetings of the Assembly. They attended more readily than the countryfolk did, especially since during the fourth century they were paid for attending, which made up for their lost day's work. These were the men Socrates liked to talk to, and whom the aristocrats despised despite the fact that they had to bow before their votes. Free men and slaves wore the same kind of clothes, were hard to tell apart, and lived alongside each other. But only the free men could retain the entire product of their work, and only the citizens had the right to play a part in the life of the city and influence its policies in any way. People have sometimes spoken of competition between the free men and the slaves. However, this poses a false problem, for the concept of competition presupposes a free labour market. Nothing of the kind ever existed in Athens or in any other Greek city, and, although some of the agricultural slaves received a wage, the only industrial workers who are mentioned in the texts as receiving one are those who were employed on public works.

Before concluding our remarks on Athenian industry in the Classical period, which we have taken as the most complete example of industrial work in a Greek city, we must deal briefly with a slightly different kind of activity, the production of fabrics and clothes. As we have seen, in the classical Greek world this was still a domestic industry. In Ischomachus' household the mistress of the house and her servants span, wove, and prepared the stuffs for making the clothes for both the slaves and the master's family. However, during the fourth century, something like a clothing industry appears to have developed. During the difficult years which followed the Peloponnesian War, some people may have had the idea of selling in the market any unused surplus from the family production. Socrates (Xenophon, *Memorabilia* II, 7, 12) advises one of his questioners to employ in this way the numerous women of his household whom he finds it difficult to support, so that he can make a profit by selling the fruits of their labour. But it would seem that there were also real tailoring establishments at a time when fashions were becoming more sophisticated and luxurious. Xenophon (*Memorabilia* II, 7, 6) gives the names of two clothiers, Demeas of the deme Kollytos who made *chlamydes* (short mantles), and Menon who was well known for the cut of his *chlanides* (woollen upper garments). While the manufacture of clothing was thus becoming a specialised profession, other operations connected with this industry, like fulling and dyeing, might be performed in special workshops by slaves under the direction of foremen, free or slave. One of Demosthenes' speeches (*Against Conon* LIV, 7) mentions Pamphilus, a rich fuller, who entertained all the gilded youth of Athens at his house, and who must have owned a large workshop. The fact that he was so rich, which is emphasised by the orator, indicates that the textile industry had developed to keep pace with the increase in private luxury during the fourth century.

Finally, this rather detailed analysis should not mask the fact that our knowledge of the way of life of the artisans in a Greek city remains vague and fragmentary. We must repeat that the classical Greek city was primarily a city of peasant proprietors, who preferred to stay in their fields than go into town. In Athens and the Piraeus there rapidly expanded a mixed population in which the citizens were certainly in a minority, but an articulate and energetic minority. Here, many small trades sprang up, side by side with larger enterprises chiefly producing for export.

In the fifth and fourth centuries B.C. Athens was a commercial city, and the Piraeus was then the foremost trading port in the Mediterranean. This trade, at least in the fourth century, was in the hands of rich merchants, Athenians or foreigners living in Athens, and they possessed ships, dealt in money, were responsible for imports of grain, slaves, and raw materials for the city. The legal speeches, especially in the second half of the fourth century, describe some of these men and give an account of their businesses and of the rules pertaining to maritime loans and the various kinds of commercial contracts. We may wonder whether these holders of capital tried to gain control of manufacture as well, rather as the Italian merchants of the fifteenth century consolidated their power by becoming cloth manufacturers themselves. However, our sources give no grounds for supposing any such thing. Industrial production remained fragmented and individual. For the slave owner, his income was often no more than a rent, not very different from land rents. For the small artisan, production was a means of insuring his livelihood by working for the community. It would be interesting to know what kind of link there was between the small manufacturers of vases in the Kerameikos quarter and the businessmen who sold vases as far afield as southern Russia. We should not be misled by the example of Pasion, who was both a banker and a shield manufacturer. Pasion made money by giving high-interest loans, and he then invested his profits by buying land and slaves who brought him in a fixed income. His shield-manufacturing workshop does not appear to have been set up with a commercial purpose: it may simply have been given to him as security for a loan.

It would be most misguided to apply modern concepts here, as has been the practice for years. The city-states of Greece in the Classical period had an economic

life but no political economy in the modern sense of
the term, and this is true despite certain attempts to
elaborate theories which do not always make as much
sense as they seem to. Perhaps it is this as much as the
lack of technical progress or the importance of slave
labour which explains the primitive character of the
Greek artisan class.

Did things change with the advent of the Hellenistic
era? Within the framework of the city the answer must
be a considered but firm negative. In the more or less
independent Greek cities of Greece or Asia Minor and
in the cities founded by the new kings, the organisation
of the work of the artisan class underwent very little
change. Proof of this is to be found in inscriptions
recording the accounts of public works, which indicate
that in Delos, Pergamum, and Athens the conditions
and organisation of labour remained similar. There are,
however, two new factors: the existence of a wider
market and of a 'royal economy'. These two factors are
intimately linked and what they imply is an expansion
beyond the limits of the city. They also anticipate the
life of the artisan in the Roman world. The guild-like
associations organised in Delos were forerunners of those
of Ostia, and moreover it was the Italians, whom the
Greeks called *Romaioi*, who made Delos the great centre
of Mediterranean commerce from 166 B.C. onwards.
This is the turning-point in the second century B.C., the
importance of which we have already stressed.

7

Artisans in the Hellenistic Cities and in Rome

THE Hellenistic age has a wealth of documentation both from inscriptions and from literature, but contrary to what one might expect, there is relatively little information about the artisan class in the cities and we are often forced to work from very slight evidence.

The social and economic conditions had certainly changed. Alexander's conquests widened the frontiers of the Greek world considerably, and one effect was to expand trade in the eastern Mediterranean. There was a flow of riches from the East to the West, needs became diversified and there was greater demand for manufactured goods. However, the well-known studies of Rostovtzeff, which remain largely valid, show that the buying potential of the great majority of the population, both in the towns and in the countryside, was not significantly altered. On the other hand, there did appear and flourish in the more or less independent cities of Greece and the East a middle class which was typical of the Hellenistic age. Even this middle class enjoyed only a relatively short period of prosperity, and its means remained comparatively limited. Only a minority were very rich—the kings with their courts, or the wealthy citizens of Rhodes or Miletus. Moreover, they used their wealth for public expenditure of an unproductive kind. Even the kings of the Hellenistic period never lived so ostentatiously as did the rich Romans of the last century of the Republic.

For this reason, in the Hellenistic period production differed qualitatively from that of the preceding period only in one respect: the production of ordinary goods to satisfy the immediate needs of the majority of the population increased little in volume, but it was now supplemented by the production of goods of a superior quality, often in pretentious imitation of artistic production which was still limited to satisfying a very small privileged minority. The new type of production, being aimed at the bourgeois middle class, which was typical of the Hellenistic cities, tended to turn into mass production.

We have particularly clear evidence in the case of pottery. There were now three different branches of the ceramic industry. First, there was the production of ordinary wares for local distribution, whose techniques evolved very little. Secondly, there was the artistic production for which Athens remained the centre right up to the end of the third century B.C., although the quality was very much inferior to that of the Classical period. Thirdly, there was now an expanding mass production of articles of fairly good quality, careful imitations of gold or silver vessels, of which the famous 'Megarian bowls' are the best known example. They were made both on the wheel and in moulds, and, as the use of moulds became more general for decorating them with relief work, it became possible to mass produce them.

Mass production with its new techniques did not bring about any change in the structure of the pottery industry, which remained a craftsman's industry carried out in many separate workshops, producing a vast number of different local varieties. In the second century B.C., however, the growing demands of the market may have led to the beginnings of an industrial concentration. Many vases, lamps, and jars found in various parts of the Hellenistic world bear the mark of a certain Ariston, and it has been thought he may have been a Rhodian 'industrialist'. On the other hand, he may well have been simply a merchant who distributed products from many scattered small workshops.

Our documentation is hardly any fuller for the other artisan industries. It does not appear that there were any important changes in the methods of mining and of reducing ore, although during this period more was known about metals, as we can see from Theophrastus'

On Mines and comparable works written by some of his students. As in metallurgy itself, there was the same kind of development as we have described in the pottery industry: the goldsmiths and bronze workers tended to make mass-produced articles to satisfy the new demand, but, for all that, the structure of the industry does not appear to have changed. The armaments industry, too, must have had to meet new demands, but again without any really significant changes. It is not even certain that there were, in the Hellenistic cities, private workshops as large as that of Cephalus, though certain royal capitals and other large cities possessed famous arsenals—Pergamum, Cyzicus, Rhodes and Sinope. Moreover, in the great monarchies, particularly Egypt, the king had no option but to exercise some control over an industry upon which depended the security of the state. No matter how close the control, however, this very seldom led to mass production, or even to standardisation of equipment. The few sources of information which we possess indicate that, as in the Classical period, the metallurgical industries were still carried out by artisans working in their small shops with a few slaves.

The same can be said for the leather and textile industries. The latter was still based on domestic production, especially in the Greek cities and particularly in the bourgeois households, where servants did the work. Only cheap clothes were mass produced. It seems, though, that there was greater diversification and specialisation in the procedures for preparing the material and especially for dyeing it. Treatises on the art of dyeing, like that of a certain Bolus Democriteus from Mendes in Egypt, indicate the level of specialisation reached in certain branches of the textile industry. Here again it was a question of meeting new demands, and it may be that in some cities, particularly royal capitals like Alexandria or Pergamum, there were large factories controlled more or less directly by the state, where marketable goods were produced by a labour force composed entirely of slaves. On the other hand, the example of Egypt proves that,

H

even in a highly centralised kingdom, small-scale artisan production continued in separate workshops in a manner very similar to that which we have described for the Classical period.

Only one industry underwent any significant development, and that was public works. The creation of hundreds of new towns, the building of ports and of roads, and the erection of public monuments intended to commemorate some great event or the generosity of some monarch, all account both for the extraordinary activity of the builders and for the emergence of theoretical writings on the art of building. These are known to us chiefly through the book by the great Roman architect and engineer, Vitruvius, who used them extensively. Hundreds of architects and engineers, tens of thousands of masons, carpenters and stone-cutters were employed by the cities and by the kings. Engineers like Ctesibius of Alexandria, Philo of Byzantium, or Archimedes of Syracuse, and architects like Pytheus, Hermogenes, and Deinocrates of Rhodes, or Sostratus of Cnidus appear both as theorists and as practitioners, and this is the only branch of artisan activity in the ancient world where there is a visible link between theoretical speculation and techniques. It is easy to explain why this was so: the construction of grandiose works such as the lighthouse of Alexandria, the Colossus of Rhodes or Hiero II's celebrated *Syracusan*, the great ship which was too large ever to enter Syracuse harbour, was dictated by motives of political prestige. And as for war machines, these were in accordance with the new conditions prevailing in Hellenistic warfare. Demand stimulated supply and set the limits of competition.

Putting such projects as these into effect probably entailed the use of a much larger labour force, and involved more specialisation in the industries affected by it. But our conjectures cannot be proved. As has already been said, the sources do not indicate any real changes in the conditions of the work itself or in the status and origins of the labour employed. It has sometimes been argued, on the basis of the greater number of known cases of slaves being freed during the Hellenistic age, that slavery underwent a decline. But really the two facts are not necessarily linked, and besides, conditions may have varied considerably from one part of the Hellenistic world to another. On the large public building sites such as those at Delos, Athens and Pergamum, although there may have existed some working teams which operated as a group, like the ones that Pergamene architects brought to Athens, the great majority of workers, whether they were free men or slaves, were still individual labourers brought together temporarily for a particular building operation.

With Rome we come to a quite different world. To start with, the little city in Latium had been primarily a hamlet of peasants. But tradition has it that King Numa founded the first guilds, and it may be of interest to record that the list included flute-players, goldsmiths, carpenters, dyers, cobblers, leather-dressers, blacksmiths and potters. Whether or not Numa was really responsible for this division of the artisans into guilds, the fact remains that the beginnings of artisan activity in Rome included the same occupations we have found in the Greek cities. The evidence of archaeology—remains of walls, urban drainage systems, and the foundations of temples—points, furthermore, to the importance in early Rome of public works, and in consequence to the existence of a skilled artisan class. Although the period following the fall of the kings appears to have been marked by a decline in building operations, these were resumed early in the fourth century B.C., in particular after the destruction of the city by the Gauls. This was when the so-called Servian Wall was built, ostensibly to prevent such a disaster from recurring. At the end of the fourth century the great projects of Appius Claudius (an aqueduct to bring water to the town; a paved road linking Rome and Capua, which was the future Via Appia) created a demand for qualified artisans. Moreover, the bronze objects found in the tombs at Praeneste indicate what a high quality was achieved by Roman bronze workers.

Obviously, we know very little about this early artisan class. Among them, there were probably some foreigners —Etruscans, Greeks or Campanians—but many were Roman citizens (who had acquired this status more or less recently) as is shown by the importance of the *collegia* to which they belonged. It was a class of free men. Although one can imagine that for the great building activity of Appius Claudius it was necessary to employ for the heavy work and the transport of materials a labour force composed chiefly of prisoners of war, it is nevertheless certain that slave labour was still extremely rare, if not non-existent, in the Roman artisan class.

The conquests of the third and second centuries B.C. initiated the process of change: both the influx of riches and a developing taste for luxuries increased the demand for manufactured goods, while, as a natural consequence of the war, the Italian markets were flooded with a skilled labour force of Greek and oriental slaves. However, these new conditions do not seem to have had such far-reaching effects upon the artisan class of Rome and Italy in general as in agriculture. It is true that some rich slave-owners did have the idea of employing their slaves in specialised crafts in some branch of production: according to Plutarch (*Crassus*, 2), Crassus possessed 500 slaves who were carpenters and masons, and he exploited their labour to indulge in various property speculations, buying at very low prices the houses which were constantly being damaged by fire in Rome, and building on their sites new houses from which he derived large profits. But this appears to be exceptional. More often the slave-owner would put the slaves to work in his house, or allowed them a measure of liberty so that they could manage a workshop or a little shop. A study of Pompeii is informative: most of the houses in this small Campanian city incorporated a workshop or a shop. Presumably the master would have his slaves work there, or he could let the workshop to a free artisan. Such workshops belonging to fullers or goldsmiths are illustrated in Pompeian wall-paintings, and decorative cherubs do not prevent the pictures from giving a very precise idea of what everyday work was like (*Plate* Ib). Mosaics in Ostia and funeral monuments confirm the impression that the structure of Italian industry changed very little during the last years of the Republic, and that the small workshop remained the normal industrial unit.

However, the increase in demand and the fact that it was easier to build up stocks of raw materials did affect this traditional artisan system in certain ways. Some industries became concentrated geographically, and also more specialised. For instance, the woollen industry was particularly developed at Tarentum and Pompeii, armaments at Capua and Aquileia, and pottery at Arezzo in Etruria. The pottery industry was producing for a larger market than a purely local one, and this entailed a drop in the quality of the articles which were being manufactured more rapidly and in greater quantities. But even when one man owned several workshops, these were never amalgamated to form one large factory employing nothing but slaves. The free small-scale artisan remained the most usual kind of industrial worker, and the great wealth acquired in the course of wars of plunder or of conquest was directed rather to the purchase of land, to luxury expenditure, to public contracts, or even occasionally to foreign trade, although these last two activities were restricted to the second estate, the *equites* (knights).

The artisans lived in narrow houses in the various quarters of the city. They were grouped into guilds whose function was more religious than professional, their purpose being to celebrate the cult that was common to the members. However, the *collegia* could also take the form of mutual aid societies, their chief concern being to ensure a decent burial for their members. At the end of the Republic, some of these *collegia* took part in the political struggles with which Italy was rent at the time. When some of the artisan groups were involved in Catiline's conspiracy, most of the *collegia* were suppressed. In 58 B.C. Clodius had them revived, but not for long, as Caesar abolished all such associations after his victory, on the pretext that they might shelter enemies of the re-established order.

What then was the situation of the Italian crafts at the end of the Republic, and what were the principal industries? The most important were the metal trades, which showed the greater degree of division of labour and specialisation. In Rome itself, we hear of pattern-makers (*figuratores*), smelters (*fusores*), turners (*tritores*), metal-chasers (*crustarii*), gilders (*auratores*), and among the jewellers there were specialist silversmiths and gold-smiths. Armour was manufactured at Rome, but also in Mantua, Brundisium, Tarentum, and Capua. The *fabri aerarii*, or bronze-workers, made table-ware with relief decoration, pots, jugs, chafing-dishes, tripods, beds, lamps, weights, scales and so on. There were also a large number of *fabri ferrarii* or iron-workers in Rome, Min-turnae, Rhegium and Syracuse.

Next in importance was pottery. The great *latifundia* had their own ceramic workshops producing pots for everyday use (*opus doliare*). Artistic pottery, on the other hand, was made in the towns, especially in Arezzo where production was constantly on the increase, but also at Mutina (Modena), Pollentia, Cumae, Capua, Rhegium and others. There were also many brick factories, for bricks were widely used for building in the Italian towns. The various crafts of the building trade were also to a large extent differentiated into lime burners (*calcis coctores*), masons (*structores*), makers of arches (*arcuarii*), builders of interior walls (*parietarii*), plasterers (*albatrii*) and many others.

Finally there was the textile industry. As in the Greek world, and for similar reasons, it was at Rome sharply differentiated from purely household production. As an industry it employed a wide range of workers, from carders (*carminatores*) and weavers (*textores*) to dyers and fullers. These latter worked in relatively large establishments situated near aqueducts. Here again, apart from specialisation within the trade, there was a geographical specialisation. Thus, Tarentum, Puteoli and Ancona specialised in dyeing and in making purple dye. Syracuse, Cumae and Canusium were famous for their fine woollen cloths, while Parma and Modena produced ordinary woollen cloths in what could really be called factories. Linen was the speciality in Padua and in Etruria, and Rome was known for its embroidery. Slave labour, mostly that of women, was often used. In some branches of the industry, however, in the production of the garments themselves, for example, free workers to a large extent took the place of slaves.

In its main lines this picture remains valid for the early Empire. However, from the second century A.D. onwards the situation changed somewhat. There was a general recession in the Italian economy which affected all sectors of agricultural and industrial life. The activity which was least affected was perhaps the textile industry in the cities of Campania, for it was a luxury industry in an old tradition. All the others were being displaced by industries in the provinces. Gaul was especially important, with its pottery from La Graufesenque and Lezoux reaching the Italian market and ousting the sigillated pottery of Arezzo. Meanwhile, there was a similar development in the metallurgical industries exploiting the rich iron deposits found in the subsoil of Gaul, in the glass industry and even in the ordinary, as opposed to the luxury, textile industry. In quality, these products were often inferior to Italian products, and in the course of time they deteriorated even further. However, the goods met a local demand which was constantly on the increase and which would appear to have been a consequence of the urbanisation of the Roman world in the West.

In all these provinces, in Gaul, Africa, Britain and Spain, the basis of manufacture was the small workshop run by free men assisted by a few slaves (whereas the East still preserved the organisation forms of the Hellenistic

105

age). The many tombstones found in Gaul, often decorated with a pictorial relief, are particularly valuable evidence. A comparison with the earlier monuments of Ostia and the pictures in Pompeii reveals the continuity of the system in which articles were as a general rule manufactured and sold on the same premises, at once a workshop and a store.

These artisans, free men by birth, or slaves who had won their freedom, were grouped into associations which reappeared at the beginning of the Empire. In the provincial cities and in Rome itself the *collegia* of artisans played their part in the organisation of emperor-worship. They also tended, more and more, to become what they had not originally been—trade guilds responsible for keeping a very strict control over the occupations concerned.

Perhaps it was partly to evade this control that workshops began to be set up on the great estates. There were already some in existence during the Republican period. But under the Empire they became more numerous on certain private estates and especially on the imperial estates which incorporated mines and quarries. This was where the latest technical discoveries were tried out, such as the water-mill. It was here too that there was some advance in the division of labour. Although some division of labour, together with some degree of geographical concentration, was also a feature of independent artisan establishments—there is the example given by Pliny in his *Natural History* of candelabra, the bases of which were made in Tarentum and the upper parts in Aegina —on the whole, real technological progress was made only in the workshops on the great estates. Examples are the mill with eight water-mills, built by Q. Candidus Benignus near Arles, and certain glass and textile factories in eastern Gaul. In the Trier area the big Gallic merchants who controlled the Moselle trade, and who left funeral monuments ornamented with reliefs depicting their various activities, transformed the glass and textile workers into genuine wage-workers. The entrepreneurs themselves provided the raw materials, which they imported, and they marketed the finished products. This type of 'domanial' industry later flourished all the more in proportion to the growing insecurity of the Empire, when the cities turned in upon their own resources and ceased to be centres of production, and the *villa* came to be a world in itself, sufficient unto itself and producing everything necessary for the people who lived there.

During the late Empire we see two changes taking place: in the first place there was a return to the economy of the big estates, which took place everywhere though more prominently in the West than in the East; and secondly, the state imposed greater restrictions on the lives of the workers. Just as the peasant was being forced into the status of a *colonus*, which tied him to the land and to its owner, in the same way the artisan found himself more narrowly confined to a trade, the tiniest details of which were controlled by the state and from which there was no escape either for him or for his children. The purpose of such coercion is clear: it was to prevent workers from deserting, and to hold them to the fiscal and military obligations which they tried to evade.

There was a special problem in the case of the artisans. The state was anxious to control, say, the armaments production or the minting of coins, in order to meet the needs of the army and to eradicate the counterfeit money which was circulating everywhere. The revolt of the *monetarii* in Rome at the time of Aurelian, the closure of certain mints and the opening of other new ones are all symptoms of a state of unease which is difficult to define. Among the compulsory guilds, *collegia necessaria* as they are termed in a rescript of Constantine, there were, alongside the workers in the arsenals and the mints, those from the weaving and spinning mills and from the dyeing establishments which still employed a largely female labour force in the late Empire, hence the term *gynaecae* which is used to describe them in the legal texts.

However, it was over the crucial occupations that the state first appears to have exercised its control: those industries which helped to ensure provisions for the army and the large cities, especially Rome. And it is in Rome that we can study in the greatest detail this supervision of the occupations connected with the food supply. The wheat supply for the city of Rome was the major concern. Although there was a free market for the surpluses which Italian landowners put up for sale, only small quantities were involved and the *praefectus annonae*, or corn prefect, merely kept an eye on the prices. In contrast, wheat which was collected by the treasury and officially distributed was strictly controlled from its importation until it was baked into bread. The emperor fixed the 'wheat ration' to be sent to Rome each year. Most of it came from Africa, and from the time that it was taken aboard ship in an African port it was the object of unrelenting security precautions. The official first responsible was the prefect of the African corn. He supervised its being handed over to the shippers charged with the carriage to Ostia. These *navicularii*, members of a guild, were kept under double supervision: during the crossing they were responsible to the praetorian prefect and the prefect of the African *annona*. Upon their arrival at Ostia or at Porto, they passed to the control of the Roman corn prefect and the urban prefect. They were required to make the shortest possible crossing and were not allowed to stop anywhere, on pain of death or deportation. They were held responsible for delivery and they paid for any loss out of their own pockets. A register of the Roman *navicularii* was kept by the urban prefect, which contained a list of the estates owned by the guild, whose sixty richest members each year contributed towards the upkeep of the public baths.

The shippers were not the only guild involved in feeding Rome. There were also the dockers or *saccarii* who unloaded the ships at Ostia or at Porto, and the *mensores* who weighed the wheat before the clerks of the corn service could hand over to the shippers the receipt which absolved them from any further responsibility. The wheat then passed into the hands of the *caudicarii* or bargees of the river Tiber, to bring to Rome for distribution to the *pistores* or bakers. That trade, also strictly controlled, was largely hereditary. In order to have his name entered on the roster, the property of each new *pistor* had to be judged to be sufficient by the patrons of the guild and by the urban prefect. A property register was kept up to date: it listed real estate, shops, animals and slaves, which served as a kind of security for the loyalty of the bakers who could neither sell nor mortgage them without permission. In the second half of the fourth century there were 254 bakeries in Rome. They were large buildings with kneading-troughs installed in the basements. Most of the workers were slaves, but there were also free men, most of whom, it appears, were convicts. The chief patron who directed the guild had the privilege of leaving office after five years. After that period he retired from the profession, lived off his fortune and might even become a senator. This indicates the importance which the bakery trade acquired from the necessity of feeding the demanding and idle plebs.

Until nearly the end of the fourth century, the bakers were also millers. But in the last decades of the century the first water-mills appeared on the slopes of the Janiculum, and from then on the documents make a distinction between the millers, *molendinarii*, and the *pistores*. The bakers were responsible not only for making the bread, but apparently also for distributing it. Under Aurelian the daily ration was nearly one and a half pounds of top quality bread. Under Constantine the quantity was doubled but the quality deteriorated, and during the second half of the century it was no longer distributed free but sold at a very low price. It has been estimated that 200,000 people benefited from these distributions. While the rations were free, the *arca frumentaria*, which was financed by the emperor and by rich senators, repaid the bakers for the expense of having accepted delivery of wheat from the public granaries. When a price was put upon the bread ration it appears that the *arca frumentaria* continued to act as an intermediary between the bakers and the consumers. A similar organisation existed for distributing oil, wine and pork, and all trades connected with the supply of food were controlled by the same strict rules. Such an organization existed on a more limited scale in the great cities of the Empire and even in small towns, and this helped to give the lives of the artisans in these towns a distinctive character.

It would, of course, be an exaggeration to generalise from these characteristics of the trades which were essential to the life of the large cities of the Empire and for the defence of the frontiers to the other trades in the late Empire. Nevertheless, eventually this tendency for occupations to become hereditary became the general rule. The aim of the system was to put an end to people deserting the towns and abandoning their trades. Imperial authorities and local magistrates exerted an increasingly tight control over all trades. The legal status of the *collegiati* or *corporati* was rigorously defined: every *collegiatus* was bound (*obnoxius*) for ever to his guild. He could not dispose of his patrimony as he wished. There were strict rules concerning marriage with a woman whose father belonged to a different *collegium*, and in some cases, for instance for the *monetarii*, such marriages appear to have been forbidden. The status of children was similarly closely defined. Finally, each *collegiatus* was obliged to perform certain duties (*munera*) which amounted to public services. These commitments could legally be avoided only under certain conditions—by providing a replacement or by taking holy orders and handing over one's possessions to the guild. Hence the many attempts at flight and the importance of the legislation seeking to repress it. It is striking that the most common sentence was to return the offender to the workshop he had left, and it was only those who facilitated the flight by harbouring the fugitive that the state punished.

As can be seen from these examples, the extension of the guild-system during the late Empire can certainly not be considered to have improved conditions for the workers in the cities. On the contrary, at the time when the Empire was about to break under the attacks of the barbarians the juridical condition of both rural and urban workers had deteriorated. This does not mean that the oppressed classes actually supported the barbarians, as we are told by the monk Salvian, in a famous passage: the example of the Thracian miners joining forces with the Goths who revolted in 376 was exceptional. Nevertheless, the arrival of the barbarians may well have appeared to many to have been, if not their salvation, at least a chance to escape from their servitude.

There is one final question: was there a decline in slavery in the crafts in the late Empire comparable to the decline in the rural economy? There is very little information on the point, and the study of the vocabulary generally used does not resolve the question, for the same word may be employed for two different legal categories in different contexts. A shortage of slaves must have made itself felt in urban artisan life as it did elsewhere, and although the women who worked in the spinning and weaving mills appear to have been slaves, it is known that the workers in the mints, for instance, were free men. Elsewhere, in the mines and in the bakeries in Rome, common law convicts were put to work. Finally, the condition of slaves and that of free men tended to merge into a common condition of servitude, in fact if not in law. And the rare revolts mentioned in our sources, which mostly took place in the eastern part of the Empire, were generally uprisings caused by hunger, lacking any organisation and without effect.

Conclusion

IT has sometimes been said that during the late Empire there was a rehabilitation of manual labour while the progress of Christianity was bringing about a decline in slavery, until then the typical form of labour in the cities of antiquity. Our analysis has made it clear that in the world of the Greek city-states, as in Italy under both the Republic and the Empire, there were always free men working alongside the slaves, both in the fields and in the workshops in the towns. Only a few occupations, like metallurgy or mining, drew their labour almost entirely from slaves. Elsewhere the slave was an assistant, a 'companion' who helped his master and often shared his frugal life. Italy alone, perhaps, developed the slave system to the full, during the last two centuries of the Republic when the wars of conquest had flooded the Italian markets with millions of men, and it was tempting to use them as labour on a large scale. During the first century of the Empire, however, the scene was already altering, and while in Italy itself the situation remained relatively unchanged, in the provinces a wide range in the conditions of social and economic dependence was to be found between the free man and the slave in the strictest sense of the term.

For these reasons slavery cannot be the sole explanation for the contempt with which manual work was regarded, nor for the stagnation in technology. Just as the city-state was maintained as a political unit even after it had lost any real meaning, once it was integrated into the immense Hellenistic kingdoms or the Roman Empire, similarly the archaic mentality, which valued effort only when it was expended in the *agon*, in competitive sports or in the game of war, lived on even after the eclipse of the society which had given it birth. Thus the idea of productive work as a form of moral training remained quite foreign to the ancient mind. The poor

CONCLUSION

man worked because he had to; the rich man left to others the task of working to support him and to provide him with luxuries and power. Christianity, at least in its early years, did not provide a reappraisal of work any more than it helped to discourage the use of slaves. The Fathers of the Church did not think differently from the contemporaries of Plato and Aristotle, and for them too work was still a curse. When ancient civilisation drew to a close, the position of the working man, far from improving, was, on the contrary, tending to deteriorate. And it was not the feudal system either which was to set a new value on the idea of work, but paradoxically the growth of capitalism which, by reinforcing the alienation of the worker, gave labour its true value, that of an activity which creates profit.

APPENDIX I

Public Works in Classical Athens

A NUMBER of surviving inscriptions on stone permit us to reconstruct the organisation of public works in Athens in the Classical period. Two extracts from these documents give some impression of the precise detail of job specifications, and of the rates and method of payment for labour.

1. Specifications for a naval arsenal in the Piraeus (347 or 346 B.C.) (*Inscriptiones graecae* II² 1668)

'The gods.

'Specifications for the stone arsenal for naval rigging [to the contractors] Euthydemus son of Demetrius, of Miletus, and Philo son of Execestides, of Eleusis. To build the arsenal for rigging at Zea. They will start from the Propylaea of the Agora, as one walks from the rear of the slips under the common roof, and the length will be four *plethra*, the width fifty feet counting the walls. They will dig the site three feet down from the highest point, clearing off the rest. They will lay a pavement on the bedrock, bringing it up to a uniform height, the whole to be laid level with a rule. The pavement is to be extended [laterally] as far as the columns, leaving a space of fifteen feet from each wall, counting the thickness of the columns. Number of columns in each row: thirty-five. The two rows are to leave space for a public passage between them, down the middle of the arsenal. In the space of twenty feet left between the two rows of pillars, the pavement is to be raised to a height of four feet, laying the stones crosswise, in the direction of the length.

'They will build the walls of the arsenal, as well as the columns, of stone from Acte, providing the wall with a plinth [at the base]. Width of the stones [of this plinth]: three feet. Thickness: three and a half feet; length: four feet, except that the corner stones are to be four feet three palms long. On this plinth and running along its centre, they will lay [a foundation of] upright stones, each four feet long, five and a half feet and one finger thick, and three feet high, except for the corner stones, whose length is to be according to the measure of the triglyphs. They will leave room for doors in the width of the arsenal, two on each end. Width [of these doors]: nine feet. . . . And on each side of the space between the two doors, they will build a partition running inwards ten feet, two feet thick. The walls against which each of the doors will open are to be built in a return up to the first columns. And on the foundation they will build the walls of stones four feet long and five and a half feet wide, except that at the corners the length [of the stones] will be according to the measure of the triglyphs. Thickness: three and a half feet. And they will give the wall above the foundation a height of twenty-seven feet, including the triglyph under the cornice.'

There follows an equally detailed description of the doors, windows, cornice and pediments, of the roof and the paving, and of the interior furnishings of the arsenal. The text concludes:

'All this will be carried out by the contractors according to the present instructions, according to the measures and the model the architect will present. And they will complete each of the works in the time for which they have contracted.'

2. Fragments of accounts of the Erechtheum (409 or 408 B.C.) (*Inscriptiones graecae* I² 373, col. 1, lines 1–45)

'South walls: length, four feet; height [   ] price: fifteen drachmas for each length of four feet, to Simon of Agryle, 45 drachmas. Length, two feet; height, two feet; thickness, one foot. To the man who laid them, Simon, resident in Agryle, 17 drachmas, 2 obols. Height, two feet; length [   ] drachmas, three obols.

'Stones forming the revetment of the portico, Pentelic stone: length, four feet less one palm; height, two feet; thickness, three palms. To the man who laid them, three drachmas each less two obols. To Simon of Agryle, two stones: five drachmas, 2 obols.

I

'Other revetments [   ] pieces in wood [   ] in Aeginetan stone [   ] of the portico: length, four feet; height, two feet; thickness, three half-feet. To the man who laid them, each stone [   ] three drachmas less one obol. To Simon, resident in Agryle, eight stones. Total: twenty-two drachmas, four obols.

'To the man who dressed these stones: fourteen lengths of four feet, at three drachmas and a half for each length of four feet. To [   ] of Collytus, forty-nine drachmas.

'East wall, before the altar. Eleusinian stone: length, two feet, height, two feet; thickness, one foot. To the man who laid them, to Simias of Alopece [   ] drachmas, two obols.

'Revetments: length, four feet; width, two feet; thickness, three palms. To the man who laid them, to Simias of Alopece [   ]

'To the man who dressed these stones on top: length, four feet [   ] obols and a half to Simias of Alopece.

'North wall. Eleusinian stone: length, eight feet; height, two feet; thickness, one foot. To the man who laid them, to Phalacrus of Paeania two [   ]

'Revetment of the gallery, Pentelic stone: length, four feet; height, two feet; thickness, three palms. To the man who laid them [   ] drachmas each. To Phalacrus of Paeania [   ] obols.

'To the man who dressed these stones on top: fourteen lengths of four feet. To Phalacrus of Paeania and his assistant: forty-nine drachmas.'

(*Note*: in this text [   ] indicates missing letters or words in the badly preserved stone.)

APPENDIX II

Ancient Monetary Equivalents

GREECE

THE drachma was the most common monetary unit. In the Athenian system the equivalents were as follows:

$$\begin{aligned}
1 \text{ drachma} &= 6 \text{ obols} \\
100 \text{ drachmas} &= 1 \text{ mina} \\
6,000 \text{ drachmas} &= 1 \text{ talent}
\end{aligned}$$

However, the most common coin was not the drachma but the two-drachma piece (or stater), the weight of which could vary from 8.73 to 12.57 gr. in silver. Fractions of a drachma were also coined as well as larger pieces, up to ten drachmas. The mina and talent were purely monies of account.

It is misleading to translate ancient coin values into modern money according to their silver or gold content. An idea of their values can be obtained only by examples of their purchasing power. Thus, one drachma was roughly equivalent to a day's pay for a man employed in public works at the end of the fifth century B.C. The jurymen in the Athenian popular courts at the same time received 3 obols per day. A slave cost between 200 and 600 drachmas, a small house in the city 2,000. In 322 B.C., when, on the orders of the Macedonian regent Antipater, full citizenship rights in Athens were restricted to those possessing property worth 2,000 drachmas or more, 9,000 men (of 21,000) fell below the line.

ROME

The Romans began to coin relatively late. Their first unit was the as, equivalent at the beginning to one Roman pound of bronze. Silver coins first appeared at the end of the third century B.C., with the denarius as the basic unit, worth 10 as, now reduced to one-sixth of a pound. The sesterce ($= 2\frac{1}{2}$ as) became the most common subdivision of the denarius.

In the reign of Augustus, the property qualification for equestrian rank was fixed at 400,000 sesterces, for the Senate 1,000,000. In the second century A.D. an imperial functionary began with an annual pay of 60,000 sesterces, which could rise to 300,000. The admission fees to a *collegium* ranged from 35 to 100 sesterces, and the dues were of the order of 5 as per month, which qualified a member to receive 300 sesterces for funeral expenses.

Gold coins were first struck not later than the middle of the second century B.C. but did not circulate widely until the Empire.

Select Bibliography

I. GENERAL WORKS

For the economic history of antiquity in general, the reader may always refer with profit to the two major works of M. Rostovtzeff, *A Social and Economic History of the Hellenistic World* (3 vols., New York, Oxford University Press, 1941; 2 ed., Oxford, Clarendon Press, 1953); *A Social and Economic History of the Roman Empire* (2 vols., 2 ed., Oxford, Clarendon Press; New York, Oxford University Press, 1957). Similar in scale is a work still in process of translation from the German original: F. M. Heichelheim, *An Ancient Economic History* (3 vols., Leiden, A. W. Sijthoff, 1958– ; New York, Humanities Press, 1964–).

The cooperative work edited by Tenney Frank, *An Economic Survey of Ancient Rome* (5 vols., Baltimore, Johns Hopkins University Press, 1933–40), quotes extensively from the sources in the original and in translation. The definitive work on the later Empire is now A. H. M. Jones, *The Later Roman Empire (284–602)* (3 vols., Oxford, Basil Blackwell; Norman, University of Oklahoma Press, 1964).

II. ECONOMY AND SOCIETY

Information on economic and social conditions can be found in the following works on Greek and Roman society:

On 'dark-age' Greece: M. I. Finley, *The World of Odysseus* (Chatto and Windus, 1956; rev. ed., New York, Viking, 1965; Penguin Books, 1967); G. Nussbaum, 'Labour and Status in the Works and Days', *Classical Quarterly*, n.s., vol. 10 (1960), pp. 213–220.

For the classical Greek world, and for Athens in particular, V. Ehrenberg, *The People of Aristophanes: a Sociology of Old Attic Comedy* (2 ed., Oxford, Basil Blackwell, 1951; New York, Schocken Books, 1962), a lively re-creation

119

of the various social classes in the latter part of the fifth century B.C.; A. W. Gomme, *The Population of Athens in the Fifth and Fourth Centuries B.C.* (Oxford, Basil Blackwell, 1933); H. Michell, *The Economics of Ancient Greece* (re-issue, Cambridge, Heffer, 1957; 2 ed., New York, Barnes and Noble, 1963).

On the Hellenistic age, see the relevant chapters in W. H. Ferguson, *Hellenistic Athens* (London, Macmillan, 1911); W. W. Tarn and G. T. Griffith, *Hellenistic Civilization* (3 ed., London, Edward Arnold; New York, St. Martin's Press, 1952); H. I. Bell, *Egypt from Alexander the Great to the Arab Conquest* (Oxford, Clarendon Press; New York, Oxford University Press, 1948).

For the Roman world, J. Carcopino, *Daily Life in Ancient Rome* (New Haven, Yale University Press, 1940; Penguin Books, 1956); P. A. Brunt, 'The Roman Mob', Past and Present, no. 35 (1966), pp. 3–27.

On slavery: W. L. Westermann, *The Slave Systems of Greek and Roman Antiquity* (Philadelphia, American Philosophical Association, 1955), and 'Industrial Slavery in Roman Italy', *Journal of Economic History*, vol. 2 (1942), pp. 149–163; M. I. Finley, ed., *Slavery in Classical Antiquity* (re-issue, Cambridge, Heffer; New York, Barnes and Noble, 1968), a collection of 'views and controversies' representing the current state of the argument, and 'Between Slavery and Freedom', *Comparative Studies in Society and History*, vol. 6 (1964), pp. 233–249; A. H. M. Jones, 'The Roman Colonate', *Past and Present*, no. 13 (1958), pp. 1–13.

III. AGRICULTURE

There is only one general book, inconveniently arranged according to the ancient authors from which its material is drawn: W. E. Heitland, *Agricola: A Study of Agriculture and Rustic Life in the Greco-Roman World from the Standpoint of Labour* (Cambridge University Press, 1921).

For the system of landholding in Attica and its evolution: M. I. Finley, *Studies in Land and Credit in Ancient Athens*

BIBLIOGRAPHY

(*500–200 B.C.*) (New Brunswick, Rutgers University Press, 1952); J. V. A. Fine, *Horoi: Studies in Mortgage, Real Security and Land Tenure in Ancient Athens, Hesperia*, Supplement IX (1951).

On rural life in Roman Italy: R. L. Carrington, 'Studies in Campanian Villae Rusticae', *Journal of Roman Studies*, vol. 21 (1931), pp. 110–133; F. S. Foster, 'Columella and his Latin Treatise on Agriculture', *Greece and Rome*, vol. 19 (1950), pp. 123–128.

IV. TRADE AND COMMERCE

No general book is available; the following, however, cover some of the ground: John Boardman, *The Greeks Overseas* (London and Baltimore, Penguin Books; Magnolia (Mass.), Smith, Peter, 1964); M. P. Charlesworth, *Trade Routes and Commerce in the Roman Empire* (2 ed., Cambridge University Press, 1926); M. Wheeler, *Rome, beyond the Imperial Frontiers* (Penguin Books, 1955); M. Rostovtzeff, *Caravan Cities* (Oxford, Clarendon Press, 1932); R. Meiggs, *Roman Ostia* (Oxford, Clarendon Press, 1960).

V. INDUSTRY AND TECHNOLOGY

Three branches of Greek industry have been the object of special study. On the ceramic industry see G. M. A. Richter, *The Craft of Athenian Pottery* (New Haven, Yale University Press, 1923), and *Attic Red-Figured Vases* (New Haven, Yale University Press, 1946); J. D. Beazley, *Potter and Painter in Ancient Athens* (London, Geoffrey Cumberledge, n.d.). On mining: R. J. Hopper, 'The Attic Silver Mines in the Fourth Century B.C.', *Annual of the British School at Athens*, vol. 48 (1953), pp. 200–254. On the construction industry: A. M. Burford, 'The Economics of Temple-Building', *Proceedings of the Cambridge Philological Society*, n.s., vol. 11 (1965), pp. 21–34.

On Rome: H. J. Loane, *Industry and Commerce of the*

121

City of Rome (Baltimore, Johns Hopkins University Press, 1938); O. Davies, *Roman Mines in Europe* (Oxford, Clarendon Press, 1935).

For the difficult problems of ancient technology, the essential work is still in the course of publication: R. J. Forbes, *Studies in Ancient Technology*, (9 vols. to date, 2 ed., Leiden, E. J. Brill; New York, Heinman Imported Books, 1964–); for metallurgy, see particularly vols. VIII and IX, and the same author's *Metallurgy in Antiquity* (Leiden, E. J. Brill, 1950).

On the relation between technology and the ancient economy, see A. M. Burford, 'Heavy Transport in Classical Antiquity', *Economic History Review*, 2nd ser., vol. 13 (1960), pp. 1–18; M. I. Finley, 'Technical Innovation and Economic Progress in the Ancient World', *Economic History Review*, 2nd ser., vol. 18 (1965), pp. 29–45.

On technology in agriculture and food production: L. A. Moritz, *Grain-Mills and Flour in Classical Antiquity* (Oxford, Clarendon Press; New York, Oxford University Press, 1958); K. D. White, *Agricultural Implements of the Roman World* (Cambridge University Press, 1968).

INDEX